Just-a-Minute Math
Contents

D0985874

Introduction

The National Council of Teachers of Mathematics highlights the importance of learning basic math facts in its math standards for all grades. The standard for pre-kindergarten to grade two calls for students to master basic number combinations for single-digit numbers in addition and subtraction. In the third to fifth grades, students are expected to master basic facts for multiplication and division. In grades six through eight, students are expected to master computations with fractions, decimals, and integers. Across all grades, the expectation is that students acquire computational fluency—the skills to arrive at the correct answers quickly—and, if necessary, that they memorize the more difficult combinations. Regular use of *Just-a-Minute Math* will help students to master these skills and to form a strong foundation on which to build higher mathematics skills.

Organization and Use

Just-a-Minute Math is divided into seven units: Addition; Subtraction; Multiplication; Division; Mixed Facts; Fractions in Simplest Form; and Fraction, Decimal, and Percent Equivalents. The tests in each unit are numbered for ease of tracking students' progress on the reproducible Student Record Chart found on pages 3–5. All units have tests of 20, 30, and 40 problems per page. Units 1 through 5 have tests of 50 and 60 problems per page as well. The number of problems on each test appears in parentheses following the test number at the top of the page.

Page 7 offers helpful information for students as they develop computational fluency—math properties provide reasoning skills to help students understand the relationships between numbers. On page 8, sample addition and multiplication tables illustrate how they can be used for computation. Math games on page 6 offer ways to practice facts in a relaxed atmosphere that can help make learning more fun.

The way you administer *Just-a-Minute Math* tests to your students is up to you. You may wish to begin by testing students for 2 or 3 minutes on a shorter test. After gauging their success, you can shorten the test time accordingly for individual students. Some students will be able to work tests in 1 minute; others will need more time.

The tests should be placed face down on students' desks until it is time to begin, and students should put their pencils down when time is called. The information at the top and bottom of the page can be filled in after the test is completed. Students may score their own or each other's work, or you may wish to collect the tests and score them. Record the number completed and the number correct at the bottom of the page. You may wish to count only those answers up to the first wrong answer as correct. This discourages students from skipping around to those they know before answering the more difficult problems. Or you may wish to give credit for all correct answers whether others are skipped or not.

The following suggestions may help students to do their best work and to avoid stress related to timed tests.

- Give the tests at the same time each day.
- Choose a time when students are alert and at their best.
- Reward students for getting all correct answers and for not skipping problems. Quality is more important that quantity, though both are the ultimate goal. For example, you might have one-minute clubs for students who have gotten all answers correct in one minute at each level. The award certficates on page 224 will help recognize students' achievements.

Timed tests are often stressful. Let students know that they should be working to improve their own individual scores and times. A little healthy competition can work well for some, but it should not be the goal. Motivate students to do their best work and to improve their scores, but let them know that these worksheets are for practice to improve other grades rather than counting as grades themselves.

Just-a-Minute Math, SV 7940-5

Just-a-Minute Math Record Chart for _____
(student's name)

Addition

Addition	Time	Date	# Done / # Right		Time	Date	# Done / # Right		Time	Date	# Done / # Right
Test No. 1			/	Test No. 13			/	Test No. 25			/
Test No. 2			/	Test No. 14			/	Test No. 26			/
Test No. 3			/	Test No. 15			/	Test No. 27			/
Test No. 4			/	Test No. 16			/	Test No. 28			/
Test No. 5			/	Test No. 17			/	Test No. 29			/
Test No. 6			/	Test No. 18			/	Test No. 30			/
Test No. 7			/	Test No. 19			/	Test No. 31			/
Test No. 8			/	Test No. 20			/	Test No. 32			/
Test No. 9			/	Test No. 21			/	Test No. 33			/
Test No. 10			/	Test No. 22			/	Test No. 34			/
Test No. 11			/	Test No. 23			/	Test No. 35			/
Test No. 12			/	Test No. 24			/	Test No. 36			/

Subtraction

Subtraction	Time	Date	# Done / # Right		Time	Date	# Done / # Right		Time	Date	# Done / # Right
Test No. 1			/	Test No. 13			/	Test No. 25			/
Test No. 2			/	Test No. 14			/	Test No. 26			/
Test No. 3			/	Test No. 15			/	Test No. 27			/
Test No. 4			/	Test No. 16			/	Test No. 28			/
Test No. 5			/	Test No. 17			/	Test No. 29			/
Test No. 6			/	Test No. 18			/	Test No. 30			/
Test No. 7			/	Test No. 19			/	Test No. 31			/
Test No. 8			/	Test No. 20			/	Test No. 32			/
Test No. 9			/	Test No. 21			/	Test No. 33			/
Test No. 10			/	Test No. 22			/	Test No. 34			/
Test No. 11			/	Test No. 23			/	Test No. 35			/
Test No. 12			/	Test No. 24			/	Test No. 36			/

Just-a-Minute Math, SV 7940-5

Just-a-Minute Math Record Chart for _____
(student's name)

Multiplication

	Time	Date	# Done/# Right		Time	Date	# Done/# Right		Time	Date	# Done/# Right
Test No. 1			/	Test No. 13			/	Test No. 25			/
Test No. 2			/	Test No. 14			/	Test No. 26			/
Test No. 3			/	Test No. 15			/	Test No. 27			/
Test No. 4			/	Test No. 16			/	Test No. 28			/
Test No. 5			/	Test No. 17			/	Test No. 29			/
Test No. 6			/	Test No. 18			/	Test No. 30			/
Test No. 7			/	Test No. 19			/	Test No. 31			/
Test No. 8			/	Test No. 20			/	Test No. 32			/
Test No. 9			/	Test No. 21			/	Test No. 33			/
Test No. 10			/	Test No. 22			/	Test No. 34			/
Test No. 11			/	Test No. 23			/	Test No. 35			/
Test No. 12			/	Test No. 24			/	Test No. 36			/

Division

	Time	Date	# Done/# Right		Time	Date	# Done/# Right		Time	Date	# Done/# Right
Test No. 1			/	Test No. 13			/	Test No. 25			/
Test No. 2			/	Test No. 14			/	Test No. 26			/
Test No. 3			/	Test No. 15			/	Test No. 27			/
Test No. 4			/	Test No. 16			/	Test No. 28			/
Test No. 5			/	Test No. 17			/	Test No. 29			/
Test No. 6			/	Test No. 18			/	Test No. 30			/
Test No. 7			/	Test No. 19			/	Test No. 31			/
Test No. 8			/	Test No. 20			/	Test No. 32			/
Test No. 9			/	Test No. 21			/	Test No. 33			/
Test No. 10			/	Test No. 22			/	Test No. 34			/
Test No. 11			/	Test No. 23			/	Test No. 35			/
Test No. 12			/	Test No. 24			/	Test No. 36			/

Student Record Chart
Just-a-Minute Math, SV 7940-5

Just-a-Minute Math Record Chart for _____
(student's name)

Mixed Facts

	Time	Date	# Done / # Right
Test No. 1			/
Test No. 2			/
Test No. 3			/
Test No. 4			/
Test No. 5			/
Test No. 6			/
Test No. 7			/

	Time	Date	# Done / # Right
Test No. 8			/
Test No. 9			/
Test No. 10			/
Test No. 11			/
Test No. 12			/
Test No. 13			/
Test No. 14			/

	Time	Date	# Done / # Right
Test No. 15			/
Test No. 16			/
Test No. 17			/
Test No. 18			/
Test No. 19			/
Test No. 20			/

Fractions

	Time	Date	# Done / # Right
Test No. 1			/
Test No. 2			/
Test No. 3			/
Test No. 4			/
Test No. 5			/
Test No. 6			/

	Time	Date	# Done / # Right
Test No. 7			/
Test No. 8			/
Test No. 9			/
Test No. 10			/
Test No. 11			/
Test No. 12			/

	Time	Date	# Done / # Right
Test No. 13			/
Test No. 14			/
Test No. 15			/
Test No. 16			/
Test No. 17			/
Test No. 18			/

Fraction Equivalents

	Time	Date	# Done / # Right
Test No. 1			/
Test No. 2			/
Test No. 3			/
Test No. 4			/
Test No. 5			/
Test No. 6			/

Decimal Equivalents

	Time	Date	# Done / # Right
Test No. 1			/
Test No. 2			/
Test No. 3			/
Test No. 4			/
Test No. 5			/
Test No. 6			/

Percent Equivalents

	Time	Date	# Done / # Right
Test No. 1			/
Test No. 2			/
Test No. 3			/
Test No. 4			/
Test No. 5			/
Test No. 6			/

Student Record Chart
Just-a-Minute Math, SV 7940-5

Math Games

Math games give students the opportunity to show what they've learned, practice their skills in relaxed ways, and apply those skills in less conventional contexts. The following games require few materials and little preparation time. You can choose or tailor different games to fit the needs of your students.

Building Math Facts

Write a math fact on the board. Pairs of students take turns replacing one of the multipliers to build new math facts. For example:

$$2 \times 5 = 10$$
$$2 \times 3 = 6$$
$$4 \times 3 = 12$$

Challenge students to see how many facts they can build in a set time limit.

Division Fish

Using division flash cards, students play Fish with three or four classmates. Students take turns asking for numbers 0 through 9. The student who is asked gives up the card or cards that have that quotient.

Math Relay

Divide students into teams. Have them line up at the back of the room with an aisle cleared to the chalkboard for each team. Place a stack of multiplication and/or division flash cards on the chalkboard ledge for each team. Students take turns picking a card, writing the problem on the board, and solving it. They must walk quickly back to tag the next person in line before that student takes a turn. The team that solves all the problems correctly in the fastest time wins.

For an additional challenge, write two- and three-digit multiplication and division problems on a transparency. Reveal problems one at a time. Team members walk quickly to the chalkboard to work the problems. Problems must be worked correctly before the next person can be tagged.

On the Ball

Students stand beside their desks. Begin by calling out a math fact and tossing a ball to a student. That student solves the fact and states a second fact before passing the ball to another student. If a student answers incorrectly or drops the ball, the student sits down. The last student standing wins the game. The game will move more quickly if you suggest that students silently choose specific facts before the game begins.

Math Bee

Divide the class into two teams. Have them stand in two lines. Use flash cards or read from a prepared list of equations. Start with the first student in each line, and have the student solve an equation. If the student answers correctly, he or she remains standing. If the student is wrong, he or she sits down. Continue reading equations, alternating teams and moving down the lines. When you reach the last person on a team, begin again with the first student that is still standing. The team with the last person standing wins the game. The game can be played using multiplication, division, addition, subtraction, fractions, or finding decimal, fraction, or percent equivalents. Or the game can be a mix of any of these.

Crack the Code

Students write the alphabet on paper and assign each letter a number. They then write a riddle and put the answer in code, using math fact answers to solve for the letters.

Math Battle

Prepare a set of cards with multiplication and division facts that do not have the answers on them. Pairs of students divide the deck of cards in half. Holding the cards face down, each student turns one card up. The student with the higher product or quotient takes the two cards, returning them to the bottom of his or her stack. If the cards show the same answer, students have a math battle. They spell out math—M—A—T—H—and turn over a fifth card. The card with the higher product or quotient takes the entire group of cards.

To let the entire class play, prepare one set of facts on paper, photocopy it, and have students cut apart the facts to make cards.

Puzzle Play

To develop skills multiplying larger numbers, students write three- and four-digit numbers on graph paper in the form of a crossword puzzle. Students then trade papers, and the partner solves the puzzle by writing the number sentence clues. When the puzzles are returned, the puzzle-maker checks the clues.

Number Games

Provide material for making a game, such as markers, poster board, fasteners, index cards, and number cubes. Have pairs of students create math games that can be kept in the classroom for students to play in their free time.

Helpful Hints for Computational Fluency

Familiarity with some basic mathematical properties can help you gain computational fluency.

Fact Families

Addition and subtraction make up fact families.

$4 + 5 = 9$ $9 - 4 = 5$

$5 + 4 = 9$ $9 - 5 = 4$

Multiplication and division make up fact families.

$6 \times 3 = 18$ $18 \div 6 = 3$

$3 \times 6 = 18$ $18 \div 3 = 6$

Commutative Property

When multiplying two numbers, the order of the multipliers does not change the product.

$4 \times 3 = 12$ $3 \times 4 = 12$

Identity Property

Multiplication: Any number multiplied by 1 equals that number.

$9 \times 1 = 9$ $1 \times 630 = 630$

Division: Any number divided by 1 equals that number.

$4 \div 1 = 4$

Any number divided by itself equals 1.

$12 \div 12 = 1$

Zero Property

Addition: Zero added to any number does not change its value.

$3 + 0 = 3$

Subtraction: Zero subtracted from any number does not change its value.

$3 - 0 = 3$

Multiplication: Any number multiplied by 0 equals 0.

$5 \times 0 = 0$ $0 \times 45 = 0$

Division: Zero divided by any number equals zero.

$0 \div 3 = 0$

Name _____ Date _____

Computation Tables

Directions: Find the two numbers you want to multiply at the top and left-hand side of the chart. Move your fingers down the column and right across the row until they meet at the answer. The arrows show 6 × 8 = 48, or 8 × 6 = 48.

Multiplication Table

×	0	1	2	3	4	5	6	7	8	9
0	0	0	0	0	0	0	0	0	0	0
1	0	1	2	3	4	5	6	7	8	9
2	0	2	4	6	8	10	12	14	16	18
3	0	3	6	9	12	15	18	21	24	27
4	0	4	8	12	16	20	24	28	32	36
5	0	5	10	15	20	25	30	35	40	45
6	0	6	12	18	24	30	36	42	48	54
7	0	7	14	21	28	35	42	49	56	63
8	0	8	16	24	32	40	48	56	64	72
9	0	9	18	27	36	45	54	63	72	81

Directions: Find the two numbers you want to add at the top and left-hand side of the chart. Move your fingers down the column and right across the row until they meet at the answer. The arrows show 5 + 7 = 12, or 7 + 5 = 12

Addition Table

+	0	1	2	3	4	5	6	7	8	9
0	0	1	2	3	4	5	6	7	8	9
1	1	2	3	4	5	6	7	8	9	10
2	2	3	4	5	6	7	8	9	10	11
3	3	4	5	6	7	8	9	10	11	12
4	4	5	6	7	8	9	10	11	12	13
5	5	6	7	8	9	10	11	12	13	14
6	6	7	8	9	10	11	12	13	14	15
7	7	8	9	10	11	12	13	14	15	16
8	8	9	10	11	12	13	14	15	16	17
9	9	10	11	12	13	14	15	16	17	18

Computation Tables
Just-a-Minute Math, SV 7940-5

Addition Table

Directions: Complete the addition table.

+	0	1	2	3	4	5	6	7	8	9
0										
1										
2										
3										
4										
5										
6										
7										
8										
9										

Multiplication Table

Directions: Complete the multiplication table.

✗	0	1	2	3	4	5	6	7	8	9
0										
1										
2										
3										
4										
5										
6										
7										
8										
9										

Multiplication Table
Just-a-Minute Math, SV 7940-5

| 0 | 1 | 2 | 3 |
| + 1 | + 2 | + 5 | + 2 |

| 5 | 2 | 8 | 2 |
| + 3 | + 4 | + 0 | + 3 |

| 6 | 3 | 4 | 4 |
| + 3 | + 3 | + 3 | + 1 |

| 2 | 5 | 1 | 5 |
| + 0 | + 2 | + 5 | + 4 |

| 1 | 0 | 3 | 1 |
| + 3 | + 5 | + 5 | + 1 |

Time: _____   Number Completed: _____   Number Right: _____

Name _____ Date _____ *Addition Test No. 2 (20)*

1	3	3	10
+ 9	+ 6	+ 0	+ 0

2	6	2	7
+ 8	+ 4	+ 1	+ 2

4	9	5	8
+ 6	+ 0	+ 5	+ 2

7	9	6	3
+ 3	+ 1	+ 1	+ 0

1	5	7	4
+ 0	+ 1	+ 1	+ 1

Time: _____ Number Completed: _____ Number Right: _____

Just-a-Minute Math, SV 7940-5

$$2 + 7$$ $$6 + 2$$ $$4 + 4$$ $$1 + 8$$

$$3 + 4$$ $$3 + 1$$ $$4 + 5$$ $$0 + 6$$

$$4 + 2$$ $$9 + 0$$ $$0 + 4$$ $$1 + 6$$

$$5 + 0$$ $$2 + 0$$ $$8 + 1$$ $$3 + 7$$

$$7 + 0$$ $$2 + 6$$ $$0 + 8$$ $$5 + 3$$

Time: _____   Number Completed: _____   Number Right: _____

0	1	4	0
+ 10	+ 4	+ 2	+ 8

1	0	3	0
+ 9	+ 5	+ 3	+ 1

2	9	2	2
+ 8	+ 0	+ 5	+ 1

3	7	2	6
+ 7	+ 1	+ 6	+ 2

4	5	1	7
+ 6	+ 2	+ 7	+ 3

Time: _____ Number Completed: _____ Number Right: _____

14

4 + 5	1 + 2	3 + 4	5 + 0	6 + 3
2 + 6	1 + 8	1 + 5	7 + 2	6 + 4
2 + 3	5 + 5	4 + 3	6 + 1	0 + 2
0 + 3	0 + 4	2 + 7	6 + 0	1 + 1
7 + 0	0 + 9	1 + 6	3 + 0	9 + 1
3 + 1	0 + 7	0 + 6	5 + 4	3 + 5

Time: _____   Number Completed: _____   Number Right: _____

4 + 4	5 + 3	3 + 6	2 + 7	6 + 1
1 + 0	1 + 3	1 + 0	9 + 1	4 + 4
4 + 0	2 + 0	6 + 3	7 + 3	5 + 3
3 + 2	4 + 1	7 + 0	6 + 4	4 + 2
8 + 1	5 + 1	4 + 5	3 + 4	6 + 2
8 + 2	8 + 0	4 + 6	4 + 1	8 + 1

Time: _____ Number Completed: _____ Number Right: _____

Unit 1: Addition/Sums to 10
Just-a-Minute Math, SV 7940-5

5 + 1	5 + 0	3 + 5	1 + 5	0 + 1
3 + 1	2 + 6	4 + 3	0 + 6	1 + 9
7 + 2	3 + 6	5 + 2	2 + 8	5 + 5
7 + 1	1 + 4	5 + 4	3 + 3	8 + 0
6 + 3	0 + 4	3 + 2	2 + 5	2 + 4
1 + 1	2 + 0	2 + 1	1 + 2	1 + 7

Time: _____ Number Completed: _____ Number Right: _____

17
Unit 1: Addition/Sums to 10
Just-a-Minute Math, SV 7940-5

3 + 7	5 + 5	6 + 3	8 + 0	9 + 1
8 + 2	5 + 2	9 + 0	1 + 0	0 + 0
1 + 9	6 + 1	1 + 3	4 + 2	2 + 8
7 + 0	7 + 2	4 + 6	3 + 4	2 + 4
5 + 3	3 + 3	5 + 4	3 + 7	3 + 6
4 + 4	6 + 1	6 + 4	7 + 3	6 + 2

Time: _____ Number Completed: _____ Number Right: _____

Unit 1: Addition/Sums to 10
Just-a-Minute Math, SV 7940-5

2 + 9	5 + 9	8 + 3	3 + 8
8 + 6	8 + 8	7 + 9	5 + 7
9 + 3	4 + 9	6 + 6	9 + 6
6 + 9	6 + 5	7 + 4	8 + 7
7 + 7	3 + 9	9 + 8	4 + 7

Time: _____ Number Completed: _____ Number Right: _____

Unit 1: Addition/Sums from 11 to 18
Just-a-Minute Math, SV 7940-5

8 + 4	4 + 8	7 + 5	9 + 5
5 + 6	8 + 5	9 + 4	2 + 9
6 + 8	8 + 9	7 + 6	8 + 6
9 + 7	5 + 8	9 + 9	4 + 7
7 + 8	6 + 7	9 + 2	8 + 7

Time: _____ Number Completed: _____ Number Right: _____

6 + 5	7 + 4	7 + 7	7 + 6
4 + 9	9 + 3	2 + 9	5 + 9
8 + 8	5 + 6	9 + 6	3 + 8
9 + 8	6 + 7	4 + 8	9 + 4
3 + 9	5 + 8	6 + 6	5 + 7

Time: _____   Number Completed: _____   Number Right: _____

Unit 1: Addition/Sums from 11 to 18
Just-a-Minute Math, SV 7940-5

6 + 8	9 + 9	9 + 7	9 + 3
9 + 5	7 + 9	6 + 9	4 + 9
9 + 2	7 + 5	8 +9	8 + 6
8 + 5	8 + 4	2 + 9	5 + 7
8 + 3	7 + 8	6 + 6	4 + 7

Time: _____ Number Completed: _____ Number Right: _____

22 Unit 1: Addition/Sums from 11 to 18
Just-a-Minute Math, SV 7940-5

3 + 8	9 + 7	8 + 3	4 + 8	6 + 7
8 + 5	5 + 9	8 + 9	8 + 4	6 + 5
9 + 4	7 + 6	7 + 5	5 + 6	9 + 3
6 + 8	9 + 2	7 + 7	9 + 9	9 + 8
7 + 8	6 + 9	5 + 8	7 + 9	8 + 8
7 + 4	9 + 5	8 + 7	3 + 9	9 + 6

Time: _____ Number Completed: _____ Number Right: _____

2 + 9	8 + 5	7 + 7	8 + 3	7 + 6
9 + 7	6 + 6	8 + 6	7 + 8	5 + 8
7 + 4	4 + 7	9 + 9	9 + 5	4 + 8
8 + 8	9 + 4	6 + 8	6 + 7	8 + 9
5 + 9	3 + 9	5 + 6	8 + 7	9 + 8
7 + 9	6 + 9	4 + 9	6 + 5	9 + 2

Time: _____ Number Completed: _____ Number Right: _____

Unit 1: Addition/Sums from 11 to 18
Just-a-Minute Math, SV 7940-5

```
    9        4        9        9        5
  + 6      + 7      + 4      + 7      + 6


    7        9        2        7        9
  + 5      + 8      + 9      + 4      + 9


    3        7        8        3        8
  + 8      + 6      + 7      + 9      + 6


    9        8        6        7        6
  + 3      + 9      + 8      + 8      + 9


    5        5        6        8        4
  + 7      + 8      + 6      + 3      + 9


    8        8        7        9        7
  + 4      + 5      + 9      + 2      + 7
```

Time: _____   Number Completed: _____   Number Right: _____

www.harcourtschoolsupply.com
25
Unit 1: Addition/Sums from 11 to 18
Just-a-Minute Math, SV 7940-5

3 + 8	8 + 8	9 + 7	7 + 9	4 + 9
8 + 4	6 + 7	9 + 2	8 + 3	7 + 6
6 + 5	4 + 8	9 + 9	6 + 9	8 + 9
9 + 3	5 + 9	8 + 6	7 + 4	9 + 8
7 + 5	9 + 5	5 + 6	9 + 4	5 + 8
5 + 7	3 + 9	7 + 7	8 + 4	6 + 6

Time: _____ Number Completed: _____ Number Right: _____

Unit 1: Addition/Sums from 11 to 18
Just-a-Minute Math, SV 7940-5

0 + 6	6 + 5	8 + 2	8 + 7
4 + 4	7 + 9	5 + 4	1 + 8
1 + 5	2 + 1	2 + 5	0 + 1
7 + 2	9 + 9	9 + 2	8 + 4
3 + 4	3 + 7	1 + 3	9 + 6

Time: _____ Number Completed: _____ Number Right: _____

Unit 1: Addition/Mixed Sums to 18
Just-a-Minute Math, SV 7940-5

4 + 6	1 + 6	7 + 5	3 + 6
0 + 3	6 + 9	8 + 5	9 + 3
1 + 9	9 + 4	9 + 7	5 + 1
6 + 2	2 + 3	1 + 0	7 + 4
7 + 6	7 + 1	4 + 9	8 + 9

Time: _____ Number Completed: _____ Number Right: _____

3	5	8	5
+ 2	+ 0	+ 3	+ 3

4	2	7	8
+ 0	+ 6	+ 7	+ 8

9	9	6	6
+ 8	+ 5	+ 1	+ 7

4	7	3	9
+ 7	+ 3	+ 5	+ 1

1	3	2	4
+ 1	+ 8	+ 0	+ 1

Time: _____ Number Completed: _____ Number Right: _____

www.harcourtschoolsupply.com

Unit 1: Addition/Mixed Sums to 18
Just-a-Minute Math, SV 7940-5

1 + 4	8 + 6	8 + 1	2 + 7
0 + 5	4 + 8	3 + 9	7 + 8
8 + 0	5 + 5	0 + 9	6 + 3
4 + 5	2 + 2	5 + 2	5 + 9
6 + 4	1 + 7	5 + 7	4 + 2

STOP　　Time: _____　Number Completed: _____　Number Right: _____

7 + 0	5 + 6	3 + 3	9 + 5	8 + 3
0 + 8	4 + 3	0 + 7	1 + 7	8 + 6
6 + 8	2 + 8	7 + 9	7 + 6	2 + 0
1 + 2	6 + 6	0 + 0	9 + 3	6 + 7
0 + 4	0 + 2	8 + 4	1 + 4	1 + 1
9 + 0	2 + 4	7 + 3	4 + 7	1 + 0

Time: _____   Number Completed: _____   Number Right: _____

31

Unit 1: Addition/Mixed Sums to 18
Just-a-Minute Math, SV 7940-5

```
   1        0        6        8        5
 + 9      + 6      + 9      + 0      + 7
```

```
   6        2        3        8        2
 + 5      + 2      + 7      + 7      + 8
```

```
   9        0        3        8        8
 + 8      + 2      + 4      + 9      + 5
```

```
   1        7        2        2        6
 + 5      + 7      + 1      + 5      + 4
```

```
   9        5        0        9        4
 + 4      + 6      + 9      + 9      + 3
```

```
   1        8        7        4        8
 + 8      + 2      + 1      + 5      + 1
```

Time: _____   Number Completed: _____   Number Right: _____

Unit 1: Addition/Mixed Sums to 18
Just-a-Minute Math, SV 7940-5

0 + 1	7 + 0	5 + 4	6 + 2	7 + 2
4 + 2	7 + 4	6 + 8	0 + 5	5 + 3
5 + 1	3 + 9	1 + 6	9 + 9	4 + 9
7 + 8	9 + 7	1 + 3	9 + 2	6 + 3
2 + 6	2 + 3	2 + 4	5 + 2	3 + 6
8 + 8	5 + 5	7 + 5	5 + 6	6 + 6

Time: _____   Number Completed: _____   Number Right: _____

33

Unit 1: Addition/Mixed Sums to 18
Just-a-Minute Math, SV 7940-5

1 + 2	0 + 4	9 + 8	0 + 0	1 + 9
0 + 3	3 + 5	3 + 9	0 + 7	1 + 5
3 + 8	3 + 1	2 + 2	3 + 3	8 + 3
4 + 1	7 + 9	5 + 6	7 + 6	2 + 6
2 + 7	8 + 2	8 + 9	7 + 4	6 + 0
4 + 6	8 + 8	2 + 4	9 + 6	7 + 7

Time: _____   Number Completed: _____   Number Right: _____

Unit 1: Addition/Mixed Sums to 18
Just-a-Minute Math, SV 7940-5

Name _____   Date _____   **Addition Test No. 25** *(40)*

5 + 2	4 + 5	4 + 2	1 + 5	6 + 2
8 + 0	7 + 1	3 + 8	0 + 9	1 + 0
9 + 7	0 + 7	7 + 4	7 + 7	8 + 8
1 + 2	3 + 0	9 + 9	8 + 6	2 + 4
3 + 6	2 + 9	0 + 1	9 + 2	5 + 0
8 + 7	8 + 5	5 + 6	0 + 4	8 + 3
6 + 9	4 + 7	2 + 2	6 + 5	3 + 4
3 + 3	1 + 8	8 + 9	9 + 5	9 + 8

Time: _____   Number Completed: _____   Number Right: _____

0	2	2	8	6
+ 5	+ 7	+ 6	+ 2	+ 0

3	1	2	5	6
+ 1	+ 1	+ 8	+ 4	+ 8

4	8	3	7	7
+ 1	+ 1	+ 5	+ 2	+ 6

8	9	6	9	4
+ 4	+ 4	+ 3	+ 3	+ 9

9	3	1	5	6
+ 6	+ 7	+ 9	+ 9	+ 6

7	7	4	3	9
+ 8	+ 5	+ 6	+ 2	+ 1

5	7	9	4	5
+ 3	+ 9	+ 0	+ 8	+ 8

5	5	3	4	7
+ 7	+ 1	+ 9	+ 4	+ 3

Time: _____   Number Completed: _____   Number Right: _____

1 + 7	4 + 3	0 + 8	6 + 5	9 + 6
2 + 5	4 + 0	7 + 7	9 + 8	5 + 2
7 + 0	1 + 6	8 + 5	0 + 0	8 + 6
2 + 3	1 + 4	4 + 7	6 + 9	2 + 1
6 + 4	0 + 2	0 + 3	4 + 5	7 + 8
6 + 1	7 + 5	1 + 3	1 + 1	1 + 9
6 + 7	8 + 7	6 + 6	3 + 6	8 + 4
5 + 5	2 + 1	9 + 4	2 + 0	0 + 6

Time: _____ Number Completed: _____ Number Right: _____

37

Unit 1: Addition/Mixed Sums to 18
Just-a-Minute Math, SV 7940-5

3 + 2	4 + 9	3 + 4	7 + 4	8 + 3
4 + 4	9 + 7	6 + 8	7 + 6	9 + 5
8 + 2	2 + 0	5 + 7	5 + 4	3 + 3
8 + 8	0 + 9	2 + 8	7 + 1	2 + 5
2 + 2	8 + 9	8 + 1	9 + 3	7 + 0
5 + 5	1 + 8	1 + 7	1 + 0	6 + 6
7 + 9	6 + 7	9 + 9	1 + 6	5 + 9
1 + 5	1 + 3	0 + 8	2 + 7	7 + 3

Time: _____ Number Completed: _____ Number Right: _____

3 + 6	0 + 3	5 + 0	2 + 6	5 + 2
9 + 4	1 + 7	3 + 4	8 + 7	2 + 2
1 + 0	2 + 4	9 + 6	1 + 1	8 + 0
4 + 4	8 + 5	0 + 6	7 + 6	8 + 6
6 + 6	2 + 8	4 + 2	4 + 6	9 + 5
4 + 8	6 + 1	8 + 3	8 + 1	4 + 5
5 + 4	9 + 9	8 + 9	8 + 8	6 + 3
7 + 8	3 + 9	6 + 4	9 + 2	7 + 4
7 + 3	0 + 0	9 + 1	6 + 5	8 + 4
1 + 4	3 + 2	2 + 0	1 + 5	9 + 7

Time: _____ Number Completed: _____ **Number Right:** _____

Unit 1: Addition/Mixed Sums to 18
Just-a-Minute Math, SV 7940-5

0 + 8	7 + 2	4 + 1	1 + 6	1 + 3
7 + 7	4 + 9	5 + 6	6 + 8	3 + 1
4 + 7	2 + 3	9 + 0	1 + 2	5 + 8
1 + 9	5 + 3	3 + 8	7 + 0	0 + 9
9 + 8	3 + 5	5 + 7	7 + 5	0 + 7
3 + 3	2 + 1	2 + 7	2 + 5	7 + 1
0 + 5	3 + 7	6 + 9	5 + 1	8 + 7
7 + 9	9 + 3	4 + 0	1 + 8	4 + 6
8 + 2	5 + 9	6 + 7	4 + 3	7 + 6
5 + 5	3 + 0	6 + 2	2 + 9	9 + 6

Time: _____ Number Completed: _____ Number Right: _____

Unit 1: Addition/Mixed Sums to 18
Just-a-Minute Math, SV 7940-5

0 + 1	2 + 4	6 + 3	7 + 7	7 + 9
3 + 2	5 + 4	9 + 3	2 + 8	8 + 8
4 + 5	8 + 7	7 + 4	5 + 3	9 + 2
6 + 5	2 + 3	8 + 6	6 + 9	3 + 5
9 + 9	9 + 5	2 + 1	9 + 7	7 + 6
4 + 8	4 + 6	8 + 9	1 + 8	2 + 6
8 + 3	0 + 8	7 + 5	8 + 5	5 + 5
1 + 7	1 + 2	0 + 9	6 + 2	6 + 7
1 + 4	5 + 6	3 + 4	4 + 3	1 + 5
3 + 6	7 + 0	6 + 0	0 + 5	9 + 4

Time: _____ Number Completed: _____ Number Right: _____

Unit 1: Addition/Mixed Sums to 18
Just-a-Minute Math, SV 7940-5

Name _____ Date _____ **Addition Test No. 32** *(50)*

1 + 3	8 + 4	2 + 5	8 + 7	9 + 9
8 + 2	6 + 4	8 + 8	0 + 4	9 + 0
8 + 6	1 + 9	8 + 1	2 + 9	3 + 7
4 + 9	1 + 0	6 + 8	0 + 2	7 + 5
5 + 4	7 + 8	6 + 6	4 + 7	7 + 7
9 + 6	5 + 6	1 + 6	2 + 4	4 + 5
9 + 8	8 + 0	3 + 1	8 + 9	8 + 5
5 + 7	4 + 1	7 + 9	6 + 5	7 + 4
2 + 2	3 + 3	9 + 3	4 + 4	9 + 4
2 + 7	9 + 1	2 + 0	3 + 5	3 + 8

Time: _____ Number Completed: _____ Number Right: _____

Unit 1: Addition/Mixed Sums to 18
Just-a-Minute Math, SV 7940-5

2 + 3	9 + 7	6 + 8	4 + 9	6 + 1	3 + 1
5 + 2	5 + 5	1 + 7	2 + 1	9 + 1	0 + 0
8 + 3	2 + 6	4 + 7	3 + 6	4 + 3	4 + 5
9 + 8	7 + 8	7 + 4	8 + 7	7 + 9	3 + 2
8 + 5	1 + 9	8 + 9	9 + 6	6 + 3	4 + 8
9 + 2	6 + 9	2 + 7	6 + 4	8 + 4	6 + 6
8 + 6	1 + 2	7 + 2	2 + 2	1 + 6	9 + 4
2 + 8	7 + 5	6 + 5	0 + 6	8 + 2	5 + 9
6 + 7	2 + 5	7 + 6	1 + 4	3 + 9	5 + 8
9 + 5	8 + 8	4 + 6	9 + 9	7 + 3	0 + 9

Time: _____ Number Completed: _____ Number Right: _____

0 + 3	6 + 8	5 + 9	3 + 8	4 + 0	1 + 5
8 + 0	3 + 9	7 + 7	7 + 1	0 + 5	3 + 4
4 + 6	3 + 3	1 + 9	4 + 2	7 + 8	7 + 3
8 + 7	0 + 8	4 + 4	8 + 4	8 + 8	3 + 2
2 + 2	7 + 4	3 + 6	8 + 6	5 + 5	9 + 6
9 + 9	9 + 7	6 + 5	8 + 9	5 + 7	0 + 0
4 + 9	6 + 9	9 + 3	7 + 5	2 + 8	4 + 7
1 + 7	4 + 1	2 + 9	5 + 3	6 + 2	9 + 5
1 + 1	2 + 5	1 + 3	8 + 2	9 + 2	5 + 0
9 + 4	8 + 3	5 + 8	9 + 8	0 + 9	4 + 5

Time: _____ Number Completed: _____ Number Right: _____

Unit 1: Addition/Mixed Sums to 18
Just-a-Minute Math, SV 7940-5

0 + 1	8 + 5	7 + 9	6 + 1	4 + 6	8 + 4
6 + 6	4 + 3	5 + 1	9 + 5	7 + 8	9 + 6
6 + 4	3 + 8	1 + 6	3 + 9	7 + 1	9 + 3
3 + 7	6 + 3	2 + 4	4 + 9	7 + 7	6 + 8
9 + 1	6 + 0	9 + 0	2 + 6	5 + 0	1 + 1
7 + 0	3 + 5	0 + 7	6 + 7	8 + 3	0 + 2
8 + 1	4 + 8	1 + 2	7 + 4	6 + 9	7 + 5
5 + 2	9 + 8	2 + 7	1 + 0	9 + 9	9 + 4
5 + 6	7 + 2	4 + 4	9 + 7	4 + 2	0 + 6
5 + 4	7 + 6	5 + 8	3 + 0	5 + 7	8 + 6

Time: _____ Number Completed: _____ Number Right: _____

3 +3	4 +8	1 +6	7 +6	5 +0	8 +5
6 +6	2 +5	9 +2	9 +5	2 +3	8 +8
3 +8	7 +3	4 +1	8 +6	1 +1	1 +5
0 +8	1 +4	4 +6	8 +3	6 +9	7 +7
4 +4	6 +8	6 +3	9 +8	6 +5	4 +9
7 +8	9 +4	5 +9	6 +1	9 +1	5 +5
2 +1	9 +7	9 +0	7 +1	3 +5	5 +7
8 +4	3 +6	2 +9	4 +7	4 +3	7 +9
8 +9	5 +3	0 +5	9 +3	2 +7	9 +6
9 +9	8 +1	1 +9	4 +5	7 +5	0 +3

STOP

Time: _____ Number Completed: _____ Number Right: _____

46
Unit 1: Addition/Mixed Sums to 18
Just-a-Minute Math, SV 7940-5

9 − 4	10 − 3	9 − 9	10 − 2
4 − 2	6 − 0	6 − 2	2 − 2
6 − 4	8 − 5	10 − 8	4 − 0
5 − 2	3 − 2	5 − 0	9 − 6
2 − 0	7 − 3	9 − 1	10 − 10

Time: _____ Number Completed: _____ Number Right: _____

Unit 2: Subtraction from 10 and Less
Just-a-Minute Math, SV 7940-5

6 − 6	7 − 7	9 − 3	10 − 6
8 − 1	5 − 1	8 − 4	6 − 1
5 − 4	8 − 8	8 − 0	7 − 6
10 − 5	8 − 2	5 − 5	5 − 3
4 − 4	3 − 0	4 − 1	3 − 1

Time: _____   Number Completed: _____   Number Right: _____

Unit 2: Subtraction from 10 and Less
Just-a-Minute Math, SV 7940-5

10	8	9	10
− 7	− 7	− 7	− 9

4	2	8	9
− 3	− 1	− 6	− 8

3	7	6	7
− 3	− 2	− 5	− 5

9	10	9	6
− 2	− 4	− 0	− 3

7	8	10	7
− 0	− 3	− 1	− 1

Time: _____ Number Completed: _____ Number Right: _____

49
Unit 2: Subtraction from 10 and Less
Just-a-Minute Math, SV 7940-5

10	3	9	10
− 0	− 3	− 7	− 2

7	2	10	5
− 4	− 2	− 4	− 4

8	10	6	10
− 6	− 6	− 1	− 8

5	6	7	7
− 1	− 4	− 3	− 0

8	7	3	9
− 2	− 6	− 1	− 4

Time: _____ Number Completed: _____ Number Right: _____

www.harcourtschoolsupply.com
50
Unit 2: Subtraction from 10 and Less
Just-a-Minute Math, SV 7940-5

Name _____ Date _____ **Subtraction Test No. 5** *(30)*

9 − 5	10 − 9	8 − 6	7 − 4	8 − 5
4 − 2	7 − 0	7 − 6	2 − 0	4 − 0
8 − 3	2 − 2	5 − 5	6 − 6	9 − 7
6 − 2	10 − 5	8 − 0	8 − 2	7 − 2
9 − 9	10 − 3	3 − 1	3 − 3	5 − 0
8 − 8	9 − 3	5 − 2	10 − 7	9 − 1

Time: _____ Number Completed: _____ Number Right: _____

Unit 2: **Subtraction from 10 and Less**
Just-a-Minute Math, SV 7940-5

7 − 3	7 − 1	6 − 1	6 − 3	9 − 6
6 − 5	8 − 7	7 − 5	7 − 7	5 − 3
4 − 1	10 − 4	10 − 0	3 − 2	10 − 10
8 − 4	4 − 3	2 − 1	10 − 6	9 − 4
10 − 2	8 − 1	9 − 8	6 − 0	5 − 4
6 − 4	4 − 4	10 − 1	5 − 1	3 − 0

Time: _____ Number Completed: _____ Number Right: _____

Unit 2: Subtraction from 10 and Less
Just-a-Minute Math, SV 7940-5

9	7	10	8	6
− 2	− 3	− 4	− 0	− 4

9	9	6	3	6
− 0	− 5	− 0	− 2	− 5

10	8	10	10	8
− 7	− 8	− 9	− 2	− 6

4	8	6	7	9
− 1	− 2	− 6	− 5	− 3

8	5	7	8	10
− 4	− 4	− 6	− 3	− 5

2	6	5	4	3
− 1	− 2	− 1	− 3	− 0

Time: _____ Number Completed: _____ Number Right: _____

Name _____ Date _____ **Subtraction Test No. 8** *(30)*

10 − 10	8 − 1	8 − 5	4 − 2	6 − 1
10 − 3	3 − 3	3 − 1	7 − 4	4 − 0
8 − 7	9 − 9	9 − 1	10 − 8	9 − 8
5 − 2	6 − 3	7 − 7	9 − 4	5 − 5
2 − 2	7 − 1	10 − 1	10 − 0	2 − 0
5 − 3	10 − 6	9 − 6	7 − 2	9 − 2

Time: _____ Number Completed: _____ Number Right: _____

11 − 7	12 − 6	13 − 7	14 − 8
16 − 7	14 − 9	13 − 8	12 − 4
17 − 8	11 − 2	17 − 9	11 − 6
12 − 7	15 − 6	12 − 8	14 − 5
13 − 6	16 − 8	15 − 9	11 − 5

Time: _____ Number Completed: _____ Number Right: _____

11 − 3	14 − 5	17 − 9	16 − 8
13 − 5	18 − 9	12 − 5	11 − 9
11 − 6	14 − 7	16 − 9	13 − 9
12 − 3	12 − 9	11 − 8	15 − 7
14 − 6	15 − 8	11 − 4	13 − 4

Time: _____ Number Completed: _____ Number Right: _____

Unit 2: **Subtraction from Teen Numbers**

Just-a-Minute Math, SV 7940-5

18 −9	14 −9	11 −4	16 −8
12 −5	16 −7	13 −9	17 −9
17 −8	11 −7	14 −6	13 −6
15 −9	14 −8	12 −6	11 −3
12 −3	13 −5	11 −2	15 −8

Time: _____ Number Completed: _____ Number Right: _____

| 15 | 12 | 11 | 14 |
| − 6 | − 4 | − 5 | − 5 |

| 11 | 12 | 13 | 11 |
| − 9 | − 7 | − 8 | − 7 |

| 16 | 12 | 13 | 11 |
| − 8 | − 9 | − 7 | − 6 |

| 15 | 13 | 12 | 11 |
| − 7 | − 4 | − 8 | − 8 |

| 14 | 11 | 16 | 12 |
| − 7 | − 3 | − 9 | − 5 |

Time: _____   Number Completed: _____   Numbuer Right: _____

Unit 2: Subtraction from Teen Numbers
Just-a-Minute Math, SV 7940-5

14 − 5	17 − 8	11 − 9	16 − 7	12 − 7
11 − 7	13 − 5	15 − 6	14 − 6	13 − 6
16 − 9	18 − 9	15 − 7	14 − 8	12 − 6
17 − 9	14 − 7	13 − 4	12 − 3	16 − 8
15 − 8	13 − 9	12 − 4	14 − 9	13 − 8
12 − 8	13 − 7	11 − 4	12 − 5	15 − 9

Time: _____ Number Completed: _____ Number Right: _____

Unit 2: Subtraction from Teen Numbers
Just-a-Minute Math, SV 7940-5

17	15	13	14	11
− 8	− 9	− 6	− 8	− 6

16	12	11	12	15
− 8	− 4	− 3	− 5	− 6

12	14	13	18	16
− 3	− 9	− 5	− 9	− 9

13	11	12	14	11
− 8	− 2	− 7	− 5	− 7

13	15	16	13	11
− 7	− 8	− 7	− 4	− 5

17	15	14	11	12
− 9	− 7	− 6	− 8	− 8

Time: _____ Number Completed: _____ Number Right: _____

60 Unit 2: Subtraction from Teen Numbers
Just-a-Minute Math, SV 7940-5

12	15	14	13	13
− 8	− 8	− 5	− 9	− 6

17	11	14	11	12
− 9	− 3	− 6	− 7	− 7

15	14	13	11	12
− 6	− 8	− 7	− 9	− 4

11	12	16	12	13
− 4	− 9	− 7	− 5	− 4

11	13	11	11	16
− 8	− 5	− 5	− 6	− 8

15	14	16	17	13
− 7	− 9	− 9	− 8	− 8

Time: _____ Number Completed: _____ Numbner Right: _____

Unit 2: Subtraction from Teen Numbers
Just-a-Minute Math, SV 7940-5

11	13	17	13	11
− 7	− 5	− 8	− 4	− 5

12	16	14	13	11
− 7	− 9	− 6	− 8	− 6

14	17	15	16	15
− 8	− 9	− 6	− 7	− 7

11	14	11	13	12
− 3	− 7	− 2	− 6	− 9

16	14	15	11	12
− 8	− 5	− 9	− 4	− 6

15	11	18	12	13
− 8	− 8	− 9	− 3	− 7

Time: _____ Number Completed: _____ Number Right: _____

Unit 2: Subtraction from Teen Numbers
Just-a-Minute Math, SV 7940-5

11 − 9	5 − 4	9 − 8	3 − 1
6 − 4	15 − 4	10 − 8	8 − 8
9 − 3	13 − 9	12 − 4	17 − 8
11 − 3	5 − 2	13 − 5	7 − 4
14 − 9	8 − 4	16 − 7	10 − 3

Time: _____ Number Completed: _____ Number Right: _____

Name _____ Date _____ *Subtraction Test No. 18 (20)*

11	10	12	12
− 3	− 5	− 6	− 7

6	12	9	15
− 4	− 4	− 1	− 8

10	13	16	14
− 1	− 4	− 8	− 6

14	7	11	10
− 9	− 3	− 5	− 3

7	6	5	8
− 5	− 1	− 3	− 2

Time: _____ Number Completed: _____ Numbber Right: _____

Unit 2: Subtraction/Mixed Subtraction
Just-a-Minute Math, SV 7940-5

6 − 2	11 − 4	17 − 8	8 − 5
8 − 3	4 − 2	12 − 9	2 − 0
13 − 8	7 − 1	10 − 2	16 − 9
14 − 9	9 − 9	3 − 0	11 − 5
18 − 9	8 − 0	11 − 7	6 − 6

Time: _____ Number Completed: _____ Number Right: _____

www.harcourtschoolsupply.com
© Harcourt Achieve Inc. All rights reserved.

Unit 2: Subtraction/Mixed Subtraction
Just-a-Minute Math, SV 7940-5

$$\begin{array}{r} 9 \\ -6 \\ \hline \end{array} \qquad \begin{array}{r} 13 \\ -7 \\ \hline \end{array} \qquad \begin{array}{r} 3 \\ -2 \\ \hline \end{array} \qquad \begin{array}{r} 11 \\ -2 \\ \hline \end{array}$$

$$\begin{array}{r} 6 \\ -0 \\ \hline \end{array} \qquad \begin{array}{r} 13 \\ -8 \\ \hline \end{array} \qquad \begin{array}{r} 4 \\ -3 \\ \hline \end{array} \qquad \begin{array}{r} 16 \\ -7 \\ \hline \end{array}$$

$$\begin{array}{r} 17 \\ -9 \\ \hline \end{array} \qquad \begin{array}{r} 7 \\ -2 \\ \hline \end{array} \qquad \begin{array}{r} 13 \\ -5 \\ \hline \end{array} \qquad \begin{array}{r} 13 \\ -6 \\ \hline \end{array}$$

$$\begin{array}{r} 10 \\ -7 \\ \hline \end{array} \qquad \begin{array}{r} 10 \\ -6 \\ \hline \end{array} \qquad \begin{array}{r} 14 \\ -7 \\ \hline \end{array} \qquad \begin{array}{r} 5 \\ -1 \\ \hline \end{array}$$

$$\begin{array}{r} 12 \\ -3 \\ \hline \end{array} \qquad \begin{array}{r} 4 \\ -1 \\ \hline \end{array} \qquad \begin{array}{r} 2 \\ -2 \\ \hline \end{array} \qquad \begin{array}{r} 15 \\ -8 \\ \hline \end{array}$$

Time: _____ Number Completed: _____ Number Right: _____

17   9   11   7   12
−9   −4   −2   −0   −8

9   10   4   10   8
−9   −6   −3   −9   −6

10   2   15   11   9
−4   −1   −7   −6   −7

12   5   8   8   6
−5   −2   −7   −1   −5

14   6   9   12   7
−7   −3   −2   −7   −6

13   15   14   13   15
−9   −6   −5   −6   −8

Time: _____ Number Completed: _____ Number Right: _____

7 − 4	15 − 9	18 − 9	17 − 8	11 − 8
12 − 7	16 − 7	16 − 9	12 − 3	11 − 3
15 − 6	12 − 9	15 − 7	8 − 4	12 − 4
16 − 8	11 − 6	12 − 6	13 − 5	14 − 6
11 − 4	11 − 9	14 − 8	6 − 5	9 − 4
14 − 9	7 − 7	13 − 4	15 − 8	3 − 1

Time: _____ Number Completed: _____ Numbuer Right: _____

Unit 2: Subtraction/Mixed Subtraction
Just-a-Minute Math, SV 7940-5

7 − 1	16 − 8	6 − 1	8 − 3	9 − 3
5 − 2	5 − 4	8 − 8	3 − 2	13 − 8
13 − 7	5 − 0	17 − 8	13 − 9	14 − 6
6 − 3	9 − 1	8 − 6	6 − 4	10 − 4
8 − 2	11 − 7	10 − 1	4 − 1	10 − 5
12 − 5	2 − 0	10 − 7	9 − 7	7 − 3

Time: _____ Number Completed: _____ Number Right: _____

Unit 2: Subtraction/Mixed Subtraction
Just-a-Minute Math, SV 7940-5

5 − 3	4 − 0	6 − 4	7 − 5	2 − 1
8 − 1	9 − 5	13 − 5	4 − 3	8 − 0
11 − 5	12 − 8	16 − 7	15 − 7	11 − 3
14 − 5	6 − 6	9 − 3	10 − 3	15 − 9
11 − 4	9 − 2	10 − 6	6 − 2	17 − 9
12 − 9	7 − 6	14 − 9	8 − 5	10 − 7

Time: _____ Number Completed: _____ Number Right: _____

Unit 2: Subtraction/Mixed Subtraction
Just-a-Minute Math, SV 7940-5

Name _____ Date _____ *Subtraction Test No. 25* (40)

10 − 8	4 − 4	5 − 3	9 − 6	9 − 5
11 − 2	8 − 2	7 − 5	10 − 4	10 − 2
4 − 1	12 − 6	14 − 8	11 − 9	15 − 6
5 − 4	17 − 8	13 − 8	8 − 7	3 − 2
12 − 4	9 − 2	11 − 6	2 − 0	7 − 3
13 − 7	9 − 7	8 − 5	12 − 3	18 − 9
11 − 8	14 − 6	12 − 8	12 − 7	8 − 4
13 − 4	14 − 7	13 − 9	9 − 3	6 − 4

Time: _____   Number Completed: _____   Number Right: _____

Unit 2: Subtraction/Mixed Subtraction
Just-a-Minute Math, SV 7940-5

Name _____ Date _____ **Subtraction Test No. 26** *(40)*

16 − 8	2 − 1	9 − 1	17 − 8	7 − 6
15 − 6	14 − 9	10 − 7	11 − 5	14 − 8
3 − 1	11 − 6	12 − 6	16 − 7	11 − 7
6 − 5	4 − 1	15 − 7	15 − 9	5 − 1
18 − 9	8 − 1	11 − 2	9 − 8	5 − 3
12 − 7	13 − 8	13 − 4	15 − 8	14 − 6
12 − 8	13 − 6	11 − 3	6 − 1	13 − 5
4 − 3	12 − 5	6 − 2	10 − 4	16 − 9

Time: _____ Number Completed: _____ Numbder Right: _____

Unit 2: Subtraction/Mixed Subtraction
Just-a-Minute Math, SV 7940-5

11 − 4	7 − 1	5 − 5	14 − 6	12 − 3
16 − 8	12 − 7	9 − 4	12 − 4	8 − 4
8 − 6	9 − 0	13 − 7	6 − 3	9 − 3
4 − 2	11 − 9	14 − 5	8 − 7	11 − 3
15 − 6	7 − 5	13 − 9	10 − 8	8 − 5
17 − 9	7 − 0	14 − 7	4 − 0	17 − 8
7 − 1	11 − 7	7 − 3	15 − 8	13 − 5
10 − 6	12 − 9	9 − 9	3 − 2	5 − 2

Time: _____ Number Completed: _____ Number Right: _____

15 − 7	8 − 3	13 − 6	8 − 6	14 − 7
9 − 4	16 − 7	18 − 9	6 − 4	7 − 2
8 − 8	11 − 5	13 − 5	15 − 9	3 − 0
12 − 5	10 − 5	14 − 9	11 − 8	14 − 5
2 − 2	7 − 4	9 − 7	10 − 3	15 − 8
16 − 9	6 − 1	11 − 4	10 − 9	5 − 2
13 − 4	10 − 1	5 − 4	9 − 3	11 − 2
6 − 3	8 − 4	9 − 6	17 − 9	13 − 8

STOP Time: _____ Number Completed: _____ Number Right: _____

Unit 2: Subtraction/Mixed Subtraction
Just-a-Minute Math, SV 7940-5

Name _____ Date _____ **Subtraction Test No. 29** (50)

12 − 5	12 − 3	11 − 3	8 − 6	13 − 6
4 − 3	12 − 4	3 − 1	9 − 7	11 − 7
7 − 5	15 − 6	2 − 1	10 − 3	14 − 6
12 − 8	5 − 4	9 − 2	10 − 7	17 − 9
18 − 9	6 − 3	12 − 9	17 − 8	8 − 5
14 − 9	12 − 6	16 − 7	8 − 1	4 − 1
11 − 5	16 − 9	6 − 1	11 − 2	15 − 7
3 − 2	9 − 5	14 − 8	5 − 2	12 − 7
8 − 3	9 − 8	13 − 9	7 − 1	10 − 8
6 − 5	13 − 4	6 − 2	7 − 4	10 − 4

Time: _____ Number Completed: _____ Number Right: _____

Unit 2: Subtraction/Mixed Subtraction
Just-a-Minute Math, SV 7940-5

Name _____ Date _____ **Subtraction Test No. 30** (50)

11	12	15	17	14
− 4	− 6	− 8	− 8	− 6

9	12	13	14	12
− 1	− 8	− 4	− 8	− 9

12	13	11	8	10
− 7	− 6	− 2	− 2	− 2

16	11	13	9	18
− 7	− 8	− 8	− 6	− 9

4	5	13	14	13
− 4	− 3	− 7	− 5	− 5

3	8	16	5	11
− 1	− 7	− 8	− 1	− 3

15	3	11	15	16
− 9	− 2	− 7	− 6	− 9

11	2	9	15	8
− 9	− 1	− 3	− 7	− 5

8	9	2	13	12
− 4	− 4	− 0	− 9	− 4

5	11	14	6	13
− 5	− 6	− 7	− 4	− 8

STOP

Time: _____ Number Completed: _____ Numbber Right: _____

Unit 2: Subtraction/Mixed Subtraction
Just-a-Minute Math, SV 7940-5

16	12	14	13	17
− 7	− 3	− 7	− 8	− 8

11	5	12	11	14
− 6	− 4	− 8	− 8	− 8

15	8	4	11	7
− 7	− 3	− 2	− 9	− 2

6	13	9	12	11
− 2	− 6	− 9	− 7	− 3

9	6	10	9	7
− 1	− 5	− 8	− 5	− 4

16	12	7	10	12
− 9	− 4	− 6	− 9	− 5

14	15	10	7	11
− 6	− 8	− 3	− 3	− 7

5	9	15	17	10
− 3	− 6	− 6	− 9	− 5

3	9	11	16	8
− 1	− 2	− 2	− 8	− 0

8	10	13	11	3
− 6	− 6	− 5	− 4	− 2

Time: _____   Number Completed: _____   Number Right: _____

Unit 2: Subtraction/Mixed Subtraction
Just-a-Minute Math, SV 7940-5

Name _____ Date _____

17	16	11	10	3
− 9	− 8	− 5	− 1	− 2

5	11	6	12	14
− 2	− 4	− 2	− 8	− 6

18	13	9	7	15
− 9	− 5	− 0	− 5	− 8

8	9	14	11	9
− 1	− 7	− 5	− 7	− 5

12	13	11	14	7
− 5	− 9	− 9	− 9	− 3

13	8	15	4	16
− 8	− 6	− 6	− 3	− 7

6	10	16	12	11
− 4	− 7	− 9	− 9	− 3

7	13	12	6	2
− 1	− 6	− 4	− 0	− 1

17	14	15	6	13
− 8	− 8	− 7	− 6	− 7

9	10	13	15	11
− 3	− 3	− 4	− 9	− 2

Time: _____ Number Completed: _____ Number Right: _____

Unit 2: Subtraction/Mixed Subtraction
Just-a-Minute Math, SV 7940-5

Name _____ Date _____ **Subtraction Test No. 33** (60)

13 − 4	14 − 7	11 − 7	14 − 9	2 − 1	11 − 3
17 − 8	14 − 8	3 − 1	15 − 7	7 − 4	6 − 3
16 − 7	9 − 6	5 − 3	7 − 5	13 − 7	9 − 1
3 − 0	10 − 2	5 − 4	11 − 6	4 − 4	14 − 6
8 − 4	16 − 8	12 − 7	15 − 6	11 − 2	8 − 5
12 − 8	6 − 1	13 − 8	9 − 2	12 − 3	4 − 2
13 − 9	10 − 4	13 − 5	10 − 9	7 − 6	12 − 5
6 − 5	11 − 9	9 − 4	11 − 8	12 − 4	18 − 9
6 − 4	17 − 9	8 − 2	16 − 9	10 − 6	12 − 6
10 − 7	12 − 9	4 − 1	3 − 2	15 − 9	8 − 3

Time: _____ Number Completed: _____ Number Right: _____

Unit 2: Subtraction/Mixed Subtraction
Just-a-Minute Math, SV 7940-5

16 − 7	14 − 6	5 − 5	17 − 8	4 − 3	15 − 7
11 − 7	15 − 9	9 − 6	11 − 4	6 − 1	16 − 9
8 − 4	10 − 2	18 − 9	13 − 8	2 − 0	9 − 4
10 − 5	11 − 5	15 − 8	6 − 4	14 − 8	4 − 1
12 − 7	5 − 1	11 − 2	13 − 5	12 − 5	3 − 1
12 − 3	13 − 7	9 − 8	9 − 2	6 − 3	17 − 9
10 − 6	14 − 5	14 − 7	3 − 3	7 − 6	7 − 4
15 − 6	12 − 9	10 − 8	16 − 8	14 − 9	11 − 9
12 − 6	11 − 8	11 − 6	13 − 4	8 − 3	12 − 8
5 − 3	8 − 7	7 − 2	12 − 4	9 − 0	6 − 5

STOP

Time: _____ Number Completed: _____ Number Right: _____

Unit 2: Subtraction/Mixed Subtraction
Just-a-Minute Math, SV 7940-5

Name _____ Date _____ *Subtraction Test No. 35 (60)*

$$\begin{array}{cccccc}
5 & 12 & 9 & 10 & 3 & 11 \\
-4 & -9 & -5 & -3 & -1 & -3 \\
\end{array}$$

$$\begin{array}{cccccc}
16 & 6 & 7 & 5 & 13 & 13 \\
-8 & -4 & -1 & -3 & -8 & -7 \\
\end{array}$$

$$\begin{array}{cccccc}
10 & 8 & 13 & 14 & 8 & 9 \\
-6 & -1 & -4 & -6 & -4 & -7 \\
\end{array}$$

$$\begin{array}{cccccc}
11 & 9 & 13 & 15 & 3 & 15 \\
-4 & -3 & -9 & -7 & -2 & -8 \\
\end{array}$$

$$\begin{array}{cccccc}
17 & 11 & 8 & 10 & 11 & 12 \\
-8 & -7 & -2 & -7 & -9 & -7 \\
\end{array}$$

$$\begin{array}{cccccc}
6 & 14 & 12 & 9 & 10 & 11 \\
-2 & -5 & -4 & -1 & -4 & -2 \\
\end{array}$$

$$\begin{array}{cccccc}
12 & 13 & 12 & 5 & 16 & 14 \\
-3 & -5 & -5 & -2 & -7 & -9 \\
\end{array}$$

$$\begin{array}{cccccc}
6 & 17 & 14 & 16 & 12 & 14 \\
-5 & -9 & -8 & -9 & -6 & -7 \\
\end{array}$$

$$\begin{array}{cccccc}
8 & 13 & 7 & 15 & 10 & 12 \\
-5 & -6 & -3 & -9 & -1 & -8 \\
\end{array}$$

$$\begin{array}{cccccc}
15 & 18 & 11 & 11 & 10 & 11 \\
-6 & -9 & -8 & -6 & -8 & -5 \\
\end{array}$$

Time: _____ Number Completed: _____ Number Right: _____

Unit 2: Subtraction/Mixed Subtraction
Just-a-Minute Math, SV 7940-5

Name _____ Date _____ **Subtraction Test No. 36** (60)

6 − 3	11 − 3	14 − 6	9 − 5	10 − 1	13 − 5
8 − 2	5 − 4	11 − 6	16 − 8	13 − 6	17 − 9
3 − 1	11 − 8	7 − 6	13 − 7	4 − 2	15 − 9
12 − 7	13 − 4	10 − 9	17 − 8	11 − 5	15 − 7
11 − 4	11 − 9	8 − 3	18 − 9	9 − 3	14 − 9
12 − 6	14 − 5	12 − 9	6 − 0	15 − 6	11 − 2
9 − 1	10 − 4	13 − 9	12 − 3	16 − 7	14 − 7
9 − 7	7 − 5	10 − 6	15 − 8	5 − 2	14 − 8
12 − 4	16 − 9	12 − 8	11 − 7	6 − 5	12 − 5
13 − 8	9 − 6	10 − 7	8 − 5	7 − 3	10 − 5

Time: _____ Number Completed: _____ Number Right: _____

Unit 2: Subtraction/Mixed Subtraction
Just-a-Minute Math, SV 7940-5

4 x 2	5 x 3	7 x 1	2 x 4
6 x 5	4 x 4	3 x 0	9 x 1
1 x 5	6 x 2	7 x 4	3 x 1
2 x 2	7 x 0	9 x 3	9 x 2
8 x 3	1 x 1	0 x 5	0 x 4

Time: _____   Number Completed: _____   Number Right: _____

Just-a-Minute Math, SV 7940-5

0 x 0	4 x 3	9 x 4	8 x 5
3 x 3	5 x 1	7 x 5	2 x 5
7 x 3	2 x 3	0 x 2	9 x 0
5 x 5	4 x 0	8 x 2	3 x 4
3 x 5	6 x 4	1 x 2	7 x 2

Time: _____ Number Completed: _____ Number Right: _____

9
x 5

4
x 5

1
x 4

3
x 3

1
x 3

2
x 0

5
x 2

6
x 1

1
x 0

4
x 1

5
x 0

8
x 0

8
x 1

6
x 3

4
x 2

5
x 3

3
x 2

8
x 4

8
x 5

7
x 5

Time: _____ Number Completed: _____ Number Right: _____

85
Unit 3: Multiplication/Facts for 0 Through 5
Just-a-Minute Math, SV 7940-5

0	2	4	1
x 1	x 3	x 3	x 4

3	8	5	6
x 2	x 2	x 2	x 0

5	7	8	8
x 4	x 2	x 3	x 1

8	9	6	4
x 4	x 5	x 5	x 1

3	4	3	9
x 5	x 5	x 4	x 3

Time: _____ Number Completed: _____ Number Right: _____

5 x 3	0 x 2	2 x 3	9 x 2	7 x 1
4 x 4	3 x 5	2 x 0	4 x 3	4 x 5
2 x 2	4 x 1	0 x 4	5 x 1	6 x 3
8 x 1	9 x 3	8 x 2	6 x 5	7 x 4
9 x 0	5 x 3	6 x 2	9 x 4	8 x 3
2 x 4	8 x 4	7 x 3	1 x 1	3 x 2

Time: _____   Number Completed: _____   Number Right: _____

87
Unit 3: Multiplication/Facts for 0 Through 5
Just-a-Minute Math, SV 7940-5

0 x 0	6 x 4	6 x 1	9 x 1	9 x 3
3 x 3	9 x 5	5 x 4	1 x 2	0 x 1
7 x 5	2 x 5	1 x 5	5 x 0	5 x 5
8 x 5	0 x 3	1 x 3	1 x 4	4 x 3
7 x 0	2 x 1	7 x 2	3 x 1	7 x 4
3 x 4	5 x 2	4 x 2	2 x 3	6 x 5

Time: _____ Number Completed: _____ Number Right: _____

Unit 3: Multiplication/Facts for 0 Through 5
Just-a-Minute Math, SV 7940-5

3 x 0	2 x 5	8 x 5	3 x 4	0 x 1
5 x 4	6 x 3	7 x 3	5 x 2	9 x 5
7 x 2	9 x 2	8 x 1	5 x 1	8 x 3
3 x 2	1 x 4	4 x 2	6 x 2	8 x 2
1 x 3	2 x 2	5 x 5	0 x 3	7 x 4
6 x 5	4 x 5	3 x 3	6 x 1	0 x 2

Time: _____ Number Completed: _____ Number Right: _____

Unit 3: Multiplication/Facts for 0 Through 5
Just-a-Minute Math, SV 7940-5

0 x 0	4 x 4	3 x 5	2 x 4	6 x 4
2 x 1	0 x 5	7 x 5	8 x 1	2 x 5
7 x 4	6 x 3	8 x 4	5 x 5	9 x 1
4 x 3	4 x 1	9 x 3	2 x 3	6 x 2
7 x 1	4 x 2	1 x 2	1 x 1	5 x 1
9 x 4	5 x 3	4 x 0	6 x 0	7 x 3

Time: _____ Number Completed: _____ Number Right: _____

Unit 3: Multiplication/Facts for 0 Through 5
Just-a-Minute Math, SV 7940-5

3 x 6	8 x 6	0 x 7	3 x 7
7 x 7	4 x 7	9 x 7	1 x 9
1 x 8	6 x 8	7 x 6	5 x 8
3 x 9	2 x 7	4 x 8	0 x 9
0 x 6	5 x 6	5 x 9	9 x 8

Time: _____ Number Completed: _____ Number Right: _____

```
    1         0         2         6
  x 6       x 8       x 6       x 9


    5         4         7         4
  x 7       x 6       x 9       x 9


    2         8         6         6
  x 8       x 7       x 7       x 6


    2         8         3         9
  x 9       x 9       x 8       x 6


    7         1         9         8
  x 8       x 7       x 9       x 8
```

STOP

Time: _____ Number Completed: _____ Number Right: _____

Unit 3: Multiplication/Facts for 6 Through 9
Just-a-Minute Math, SV 7940-5

3	6	9	6
x 7	x 6	x 9	x 9

8	7	5	1
x 6	x 9	x 8	x 9

2	4	7	0
x 8	x 8	x 6	x 6

0	3	4	6
x 8	x 6	x 7	x 7

2	1	4	7
x 7	x 8	x 9	x 8

Time: _____ Number Completed: _____ Number Right: _____

1	7	3	7
x 6	x 7	x 9	x 6

8	4	0	8
x 7	x 6	x 7	x 8

6	5	2	5
x 8	x 7	x 6	x 9

0	3	5	9
x 9	x 8	x 6	x 8

1	8	9	2
x 7	x 9	x 7	x 9

Time: _____ Number Completed: _____ Number Right: _____

94
Unit 3: Multiplication/Facts for 6 Through 9
Just-a-Minute Math, SV 7940-5

0 x 7	4 x 7	7 x 7	7 x 8	8 x 6
6 x 6	7 x 6	8 x 8	3 x 9	9 x 6
9 x 8	1 x 7	2 x 8	6 x 7	5 x 8
5 x 9	8 x 9	5 x 6	9 x 7	2 x 9
3 x 6	0 x 8	7 x 9	6 x 9	9 x 9
1 x 9	1 x 6	0 x 6	0 x 9	1 x 8

Time: _____ Number Completed: _____ Number Right: _____

2	4	9	9	5
x 6	x 6	x 8	x 9	x 8

5	3	4	5	2
x 7	x 7	x 7	x 6	x 8

4	4	6	7	9
x 9	x 8	x 6	x 8	x 7

2	6	3	6	8
x 7	x 8	x 6	x 7	x 9

8	0	1	8	1
x 7	x 7	x 8	x 6	x 6

3	7	6	0	2
x 8	x 9	x 9	x 8	x 9

Time: _____ Number Completed: _____ Number Right: _____

Unit 3: Multiplication/Facts for 6 Through 9
Just-a-Minute Math, SV 7940-5

0 x 6	4 x 6	5 x 7	9 x 6	7 x 9
4 x 8	7 x 7	1 x 7	2 x 7	2 x 8
5 x 9	8 x 7	2 x 6	9 x 7	5 x 6
3 x 9	6 x 8	3 x 8	6 x 9	1 x 8
7 x 6	4 x 9	0 x 9	0 x 8	9 x 9
8 x 8	1 x 9	3 x 7	6 x 6	3 x 6

Time: _____ Number Completed: _____ Number Right: _____

Unit 3: Multiplication/Facts for 6 Through 9
Just-a-Minute Math, SV 7940-5

7
x 7

8
x 9

0
x 9

8
x 7

3
x 7

9
x 8

5
x 9

1
x 6

1
x 9

2
x 7

3
x 9

1
x 7

4
x 9

0
x 6

6
x 8

0
x 7

6
x 7

8
x 8

5
x 7

4
x 7

2
x 6

4
x 6

3
x 6

4
x 8

5
x 8

9
x 6

7
x 6

8
x 6

7
x 8

2
x 9

Time: _____ Number Completed: _____ Number Right: _____

Unit 3: Multiplication/Facts for 6 Through 9
Just-a-Minute Math, SV 7940-5

1	5	7	8
x 0	x 7	x 2	x 9

7	9	6	2
x 5	x 8	x 1	x 8

4	3	5	5
x 3	x 7	x 0	x 8

0	5	2	7
x 5	x 5	x 2	x 3

9	3	9	0
x 3	x 4	x 5	x 7

Time: _____ Number Completed: _____ Number Right: _____

Name _____ Date _____ **Multiplication Test No. 18 (20)**

2 x 5	4 x 7	0 x 9	6 x 7
5 x 6	5 x 2	4 x 4	3 x 5
6 x 3	5 x 4	1 x 3	7 x 6
4 x 2	8 x 6	8 x 4	3 x 3
9 x 2	6 x 9	7 x 0	8 x 5

Time: _____ Number Completed: _____ Number Right: _____

Unit 3: Multiplication/Mixed Facts for 0 Through 9
Just-a-Minute Math, SV 7940-5

1	1	6	7
x 6	x 1	x 6	x 1

6	8	4	0
x 2	x 2	x 8	x 3

7	6	9	7
x 8	x 4	x 6	x 9

3	5	7	2
x 8	x 3	x 4	x 9

6	8	2	6
x 5	x 1	x 4	x 0

Time: _____ Number Completed: _____ Number Right: _____

6 x 8	8 x 3	2 x 7	8 x 8
2 x 1	0 x 1	0 x 0	2 x 3
8 x 0	4 x 9	1 x 4	5 x 1
9 x 7	7 x 7	9 x 9	3 x 6
1 x 8	9 x 4	4 x 5	3 x 9

Time: _____ Number Completed: _____ Number Right: _____

www.harcourtschoolsupply.com

102

Unit 3: Multiplication/Mixed Facts for 0 Through 9
Just-a-Minute Math, SV 7940-5

0 x 2	9 x 0	3 x 1	3 x 3	6 x 4
1 x 5	4 x 6	0 x 4	6 x 8	3 x 4
8 x 7	5 x 9	6 x 9	4 x 3	9 x 3
9 x 8	4 x 0	1 x 8	6 x 6	2 x 2
0 x 8	2 x 6	7 x 4	7 x 9	4 x 9
3 x 2	1 x 9	9 x 7	0 x 6	7 x 6

Time: _____ Number Completed: _____ Number Right: _____

6	2	2	1	3
x 7	x 5	x 3	x 7	x 9

1	4	9	8	7
x 3	x 2	x 6	x 2	x 2

6	8	9	0	1
x 2	x 4	x 9	x 7	x 4

7	9	0	2	8
x 7	x 5	x 0	x 1	x 6

3	2	9	9	6
x 8	x 7	x 4	x 2	x 3

4	7	6	2	5
x 8	x 1	x 5	x 4	x 3

Time: _____ Number Completed: _____ Number Right: _____

www.harcourtschoolsupply.com
© Harcourt Achieve Inc. All rights reserved.

Unit 3: Multiplication/Mixed Facts for 0 Through 9
Just-a-Minute Math, SV 7940-5

5 x 8	5 x 2	1 x 1	7 x 3	4 x 5
2 x 8	8 x 1	8 x 9	8 x 8	3 x 5
7 x 5	5 x 7	7 x 8	4 x 4	5 x 5
3 x 6	2 x 9	5 x 6	3 x 7	4 x 7
0 x 3	0 x 5	1 x 2	0 x 9	5 x 4
8 x 5	5 x 1	9 x 1	4 x 1	8 x 3

Time: _____ Number Completed: _____ Number Right: _____

5	7	3	8	4
x 4	x 3	x 6	x 2	x 7

7	6	6	9	0
x 7	x 2	x 4	x 8	x 2

2	2	9	9	3
x 8	x 2	x 3	x 9	x 1

8	9	5	5	8
x 5	x 6	x 2	x 8	x 3

1	8	3	5	8
x 5	x 8	x 3	x 6	x 4

0	4	1	3	4
x 4	x 8	x 1	x 4	x 2

Time: _____ Number Completed: _____ Number Right: _____

106

Unit 3: Multiplication/Mixed Facts for 0 Through 9
Just-a-Minute Math, SV 7940-5

3 x 0	8 x 7	8 x 1	2 x 5	6 x 6
7 x 6	1 x 3	1 x 2	9 x 7	7 x 4
4 x 9	7 x 0	7 x 9	6 x 8	7 x 2
1 x 7	9 x 5	8 x 9	5 x 9	7 x 8
9 x 4	4 x 5	1 x 8	2 x 6	3 x 9
4 x 3	0 x 5	9 x 2	1 x 4	1 x 6
5 x 7	6 x 9	3 x 2	0 x 9	6 x 5
2 x 9	5 x 3	7 x 3	3 x 5	2 x 4

Time: _____ Number Completed: _____ Number Right: _____

Unit 3: Multiplication/Mixed Facts for 0 Through 9
Just-a-Minute Math, SV 7940-5

Name _____ Date _____ *Multiplication Test No. 26* (40)

3 x 8	4 x 4	2 x 0	0 x 8	9 x 5
3 x 7	2 x 3	4 x 7	5 x 0	2 x 9
7 x 5	6 x 1	8 x 8	9 x 2	7 x 4
0 x 1	0 x 0	6 x 6	0 x 7	9 x 9
6 x 7	7 x 1	2 x 4	8 x 7	5 x 4
1 x 9	4 x 6	8 x 3	4 x 8	7 x 2
2 x 7	8 x 6	4 x 2	6 x 9	3 x 3
5 x 5	9 x 1	9 x 4	5 x 2	4 x 9

STOP

Time: _____ Number Completed: _____ Number Right: _____

Unit 3: Multiplication/Mixed Facts for 0 Through 9
Just-a-Minute Math, SV 7940-5

8 x 5	7 x 9	1 x 4	3 x 2	9 x 6
6 x 8	1 x 8	2 x 8	1 x 2	4 x 5
0 x 9	2 x 2	8 x 2	5 x 8	5 x 7
4 x 1	7 x 7	4 x 3	3 x 6	9 x 7
9 x 3	1 x 7	8 x 9	8 x 4	2 x 5
7 x 0	5 x 9	3 x 9	6 x 5	7 x 3
0 x 6	7 x 7	5 x 6	3 x 5	6 x 2
9 x 8	6 x 3	2 x 6	7 x 8	3 x 4

Time: _____ Number Completed: _____ Number Right: _____

109

Unit 3: Multiplication/Mixed Facts for 0 Through 9
Just-a-Minute Math, SV 7940-5

1 x 5	5 x 9	1 x 9	5 x 1	9 x 3
7 x 7	5 x 2	3 x 8	3 x 1	8 x 9
2 x 1	1 x 1	3 x 7	0 x 0	7 x 6
5 x 7	9 x 0	4 x 6	4 x 8	9 x 4
2 x 9	4 x 1	5 x 5	6 x 9	6 x 4
9 x 8	8 x 8	7 x 5	9 x 5	3 x 5
8 x 2	5 x 6	4 x 4	8 x 3	6 x 5
6 x 7	8 x 6	2 x 3	4 x 2	3 x 3

STOP

Time: _____ Number Completed: _____ Number Right: _____

Unit 3: Multiplication/Mixed Facts for 0 Through 9
Just-a-Minute Math, SV 7940-5

2	1	6	9	9
x 1	x 0	x 4	x 6	x 9

5	9	0	2	3
x 5	x 5	x 0	x 4	x 0

8	6	9	0	7
x 9	x 3	x 2	x 7	x 6

3	2	6	7	3
x 6	x 5	x 8	x 5	x 8

4	3	1	9	5
x 4	x 9	x 7	x 3	x 4

8	0	9	4	9
x 3	x 6	x 4	x 6	x 8

5	8	2	3	3
x 2	x 4	x 6	x 7	x 3

8	5	1	4	2
x 1	x 6	x 3	x 9	x 2

2	4	7	0	7
x 8	x 8	x 0	x 9	x 2

7	6	5	8	8
x 7	x 9	x 8	x 5	x 8

Time: _____ Number Completed: _____ Number Right: _____

Unit 3: Multiplication/Mixed Facts for 0 Through 9
Just-a-Minute Math, SV 7940-5

0 x 5	2 x 9	1 x 9	3 x 5	9 x 8
3 x 4	0 x 8	4 x 1	0 x 1	4 x 8
7 x 4	4 x 0	4 x 5	5 x 3	9 x 5
8 x 6	6 x 5	4 x 7	9 x 1	7 x 7
7 x 9	5 x 9	7 x 8	7 x 3	3 x 9
1 x 6	2 x 7	8 x 2	3 x 2	8 x 9
0 x 2	1 x 8	6 x 1	6 x 0	2 x 4
8 x 7	5 x 0	4 x 3	2 x 0	6 x 8
5 x 7	1 x 5	6 x 6	6 x 2	0 x 3
6 x 7	9 x 7	8 x 0	7 x 6	7 x 1

Time: _____ Number Completed: _____ Number Right: _____

112
Unit 3: Multiplication/Mixed Facts for 0 Through 9
Just-a-Minute Math, SV 7940-5

Name _____ Date _____ **Multiplication Test No. 31** *(50)*

1 x 1	9 x 2	1 x 9	9 x 3	8 x 8
6 x 7	5 x 1	0 x 4	7 x 6	1 x 3
2 x 8	4 x 2	1 x 2	2 x 7	4 x 6
7 x 3	6 x 6	6 x 4	5 x 2	7 x 2
9 x 5	3 x 9	6 x 8	3 x 1	9 x 7
6 x 9	2 x 6	4 x 8	5 x 8	9 x 9
6 x 5	5 x 4	8 x 5	2 x 5	5 x 9
3 x 6	3 x 3	4 x 5	8 x 3	3 x 5
6 x 3	2 x 2	7 x 4	9 x 4	8 x 4
2 x 3	8 x 9	4 x 3	1 x 7	9 x 6

Time: _____ Number Completed: _____ Number Right: _____

Unit 3: Multiplication/Mixed Facts for 0 Through 9
Just-a-Minute Math, SV 7940-5

6 x 2	8 x 2	3 x 0	6 x 8	7 x 3
5 x 8	3 x 2	3 x 7	4 x 4	4 x 5
5 x 3	1 x 6	7 x 7	4 x 2	2 x 3
1 x 4	4 x 7	8 x 7	2 x 9	6 x 1
7 x 1	7 x 8	3 x 8	9 x 4	2 x 2
9 x 0	9 x 8	4 x 1	9 x 9	8 x 9
0 x 4	8 x 6	1 x 8	5 x 9	9 x 7
4 x 9	5 x 6	5 x 5	7 x 8	6 x 6
7 x 9	3 x 4	9 x 1	1 x 7	8 x 4
7 x 5	8 x 1	5 x 7	0 x 3	6 x 4

Time: _____ Number Completed: _____ Number Right: _____

Unit 3: Multiplication/Mixed Facts for 0 Through 9
Just-a-Minute Math, SV 7940-5

3 x 8	5 x 6	8 x 8	2 x 8	1 x 2	9 x 5
6 x 7	8 x 3	2 x 9	5 x 1	4 x 7	9 x 3
7 x 4	9 x 6	1 x 6	1 x 0	3 x 7	2 x 6
6 x 1	6 x 9	4 x 4	7 x 7	7 x 5	4 x 3
0 x 7	2 x 7	6 x 3	3 x 9	8 x 2	5 x 0
3 x 2	9 x 8	3 x 6	4 x 8	1 x 3	1 x 5
8 x 7	4 x 6	8 x 6	7 x 6	2 x 5	7 x 3
4 x 9	3 x 5	5 x 5	5 x 3	6 x 5	9 x 7
1 x 8	5 x 2	4 x 2	6 x 2	5 x 4	5 x 7
7 x 2	9 x 2	7 x 9	9 x 1	8 x 1	2 x 4

STOP

Time: _____ Number Completed: _____ Number Right: _____

Name _____ Date _____

5 x 6	7 x 9	9 x 9	0 x 7	9 x 4	6 x 6
8 x 7	8 x 6	5 x 8	2 x 2	6 x 3	8 x 4
4 x 9	6 x 7	5 x 7	5 x 1	4 x 5	7 x 1
7 x 4	4 x 6	2 x 5	6 x 0	0 x 2	3 x 9
2 x 7	9 x 3	7 x 3	5 x 5	8 x 2	7 x 6
0 x 4	2 x 9	1 x 3	7 x 8	8 x 9	4 x 8
3 x 5	9 x 5	5 x 3	0 x 8	3 x 7	5 x 4
3 x 3	1 x 6	3 x 1	7 x 5	4 x 3	4 x 2
7 x 2	6 x 2	3 x 8	3 x 6	9 x 6	8 x 1
0 x 0	3 x 4	9 x 8	2 x 4	0 x 9	9 x 2

Time: _____ Number Completed: _____ Number Right: _____

Unit 3: Multiplication/Mixed Facts for 0 Through 9
Just-a-Minute Math, SV 7940-5

Name _____ Date _____

6 x 8	2 x 3	8 x 3	4 x 6	1 x 9	9 x 5
6 x 5	6 x 1	4 x 4	7 x 6	3 x 2	3 x 7
5 x 9	3 x 0	1 x 1	9 x 8	2 x 1	2 x 2
2 x 6	1 x 7	5 x 0	1 x 0	1 x 4	5 x 3
0 x 5	2 x 8	9 x 2	9 x 4	7 x 8	9 x 9
9 x 7	6 x 4	1 x 5	8 x 8	8 x 0	3 x 3
6 x 9	5 x 2	1 x 2	9 x 1	6 x 7	5 x 6
1 x 8	4 x 1	7 x 2	2 x 0	8 x 9	8 x 4
4 x 7	7 x 7	9 x 6	4 x 8	2 x 7	4 x 5
8 x 5	0 x 6	7 x 9	8 x 7	7 x 0	8 x 2

Time: _____ Number Completed: _____ Number Right: _____

2 x 9	4 x 2	7 x 1	6 x 2	6 x 5	5 x 3
4 x 4	0 x 0	2 x 4	1 x 3	3 x 2	8 x 8
6 x 9	6 x 4	5 x 8	4 x 9	8 x 1	4 x 5
6 x 3	3 x 4	8 x 8	3 x 8	4 x 0	8 x 4
4 x 1	9 x 0	5 x 2	6 x 6	5 x 7	9 x 4
2 x 5	5 x 9	9 x 1	7 x 5	7 x 4	5 x 6
6 x 8	3 x 9	9 x 7	7 x 3	4 x 7	9 x 5
8 x 5	5 x 5	7 x 7	2 x 3	0 x 3	9 x 8
5 x 4	8 x 6	3 x 6	5 x 1	8 x 3	9 x 9
9 x 3	2 x 6	4 x 3	3 x 5	1 x 6	7 x 2

Time: _____ Number Completed: _____ Number Right: _____

118

Unit 3: Multiplication/Mixed Facts for 0 Through 9

Just-a-Minute Math, SV 7940-5

$1\overline{)5}$ $4\overline{)24}$ $2\overline{)18}$ $1\overline{)8}$

$2\overline{)10}$ $2\overline{)14}$ $3\overline{)9}$ $4\overline{)36}$

$3\overline{)27}$ $2\overline{)0}$ $1\overline{)3}$ $3\overline{)24}$

$5\overline{)0}$ $3\overline{)12}$ $4\overline{)16}$ $2\overline{)4}$

$5\overline{)25}$ $5\overline{)10}$ $3\overline{)18}$ $1\overline{)1}$

Time: _____   Number Completed: _____   Number Right: _____

$2\overline{)16}$ $\qquad$ $2\overline{)0}$ $\qquad$ $4\overline{)8}$ $\qquad$ $2\overline{)8}$

$3\overline{)0}$ $\qquad$ $5\overline{)30}$ $\qquad$ $2\overline{)12}$ $\qquad$ $3\overline{)6}$

$4\overline{)28}$ $\qquad$ $3\overline{)21}$ $\qquad$ $3\overline{)3}$ $\qquad$ $4\overline{)32}$

$3\overline{)15}$ $\qquad$ $1\overline{)7}$ $\qquad$ $4\overline{)20}$ $\qquad$ $5\overline{)45}$

$1\overline{)1}$ $\qquad$ $5\overline{)15}$ $\qquad$ $5\overline{)40}$ $\qquad$ $4\overline{)4}$

Time: _____ Number Completed: _____ Number Right: _____

$5\overline{)5}$ $5\overline{)35}$ $1\overline{)2}$ $3\overline{)27}$

$4\overline{)12}$ $2\overline{)2}$ $4\overline{)0}$ $2\overline{)18}$

$2\overline{)6}$ $1\overline{)9}$ $1\overline{)6}$ $2\overline{)14}$

$3\overline{)0}$ $2\overline{)0}$ $3\overline{)18}$ $4\overline{)24}$

$1\overline{)4}$ $5\overline{)20}$ $5\overline{)30}$ $5\overline{)40}$

STOP

Time: _____ Number Completed: _____ Number Right: _____

Unit 4: Division/Facts for 1 Through 5
Just-a-Minute Math, SV 7940-5

$2\overline{)16}$ $4\overline{)28}$ $4\overline{)20}$ $3\overline{)0}$

$4\overline{)16}$ $3\overline{)12}$ $5\overline{)35}$ $5\overline{)45}$

$3\overline{)9}$ $2\overline{)12}$ $4\overline{)8}$ $3\overline{)24}$

$5\overline{)15}$ $5\overline{)10}$ $4\overline{)32}$ $2\overline{)8}$

$1\overline{)7}$ $1\overline{)8}$ $3\overline{)21}$ $3\overline{)3}$

Time: _____ Number Completed: _____ Number Right: _____

$1\overline{)3}$ $4\overline{)4}$ $5\overline{)0}$ $3\overline{)24}$ $4\overline{)0}$

$5\overline{)25}$ $5\overline{)20}$ $1\overline{)4}$ $1\overline{)9}$ $2\overline{)0}$

$5\overline{)5}$ $4\overline{)36}$ $1\overline{)2}$ $4\overline{)16}$ $5\overline{)40}$

$3\overline{)15}$ $2\overline{)10}$ $3\overline{)21}$ $2\overline{)14}$ $3\overline{)18}$

$3\overline{)0}$ $2\overline{)4}$ $5\overline{)35}$ $3\overline{)12}$ $2\overline{)8}$

$2\overline{)6}$ $3\overline{)6}$ $2\overline{)16}$ $4\overline{)24}$ $5\overline{)15}$

STOP Time: _____ Number Completed: _____ Number Right: _____

$1\overline{)6}$ $4\overline{)36}$ $2\overline{)6}$ $4\overline{)28}$ $2\overline{)12}$

$3\overline{)21}$ $5\overline{)15}$ $5\overline{)5}$ $3\overline{)15}$ $5\overline{)10}$

$4\overline{)8}$ $3\overline{)9}$ $2\overline{)10}$ $2\overline{)0}$ $2\overline{)2}$

$2\overline{)18}$ $1\overline{)0}$ $5\overline{)25}$ $5\overline{)20}$ $3\overline{)18}$

$5\overline{)45}$ $4\overline{)16}$ $2\overline{)14}$ $1\overline{)4}$ $4\overline{)12}$

$4\overline{)0}$ $3\overline{)27}$ $3\overline{)0}$ $4\overline{)24}$ $1\overline{)8}$

Time: _____   Number Completed: _____   Number Right: _____

Just-a-Minute Math, SV 7940-5

$4\overline{)20}$ $2\overline{)16}$ $4\overline{)32}$ $4\overline{)8}$ $2\overline{)18}$

$5\overline{)35}$ $4\overline{)4}$ $5\overline{)30}$ $5\overline{)20}$ $1\overline{)7}$

$3\overline{)24}$ $3\overline{)6}$ $5\overline{)0}$ $1\overline{)9}$ $5\overline{)15}$

$1\overline{)1}$ $4\overline{)0}$ $1\overline{)2}$ $2\overline{)8}$ $3\overline{)9}$

$2\overline{)0}$ $1\overline{)5}$ $3\overline{)3}$ $4\overline{)36}$ $1\overline{)3}$

$5\overline{)40}$ $3\overline{)12}$ $3\overline{)27}$ $5\overline{)25}$ $4\overline{)28}$

Time: _____ Number Completed: _____ Number Right: _____

125   Unit 4: Division/Facts for 1 Through 5
Just-a-Minute Math, SV 7940-5

$2\overline{)14}$ $3\overline{)24}$ $2\overline{)8}$ $3\overline{)18}$ $2\overline{)12}$

$5\overline{)30}$ $2\overline{)10}$ $5\overline{)40}$ $3\overline{)6}$ $4\overline{)16}$

$1\overline{)0}$ $1\overline{)5}$ $3\overline{)21}$ $3\overline{)0}$ $5\overline{)10}$

$2\overline{)16}$ $2\overline{)4}$ $4\overline{)20}$ $1\overline{)2}$ $2\overline{)18}$

$1\overline{)4}$ $3\overline{)12}$ $5\overline{)35}$ $5\overline{)45}$ $4\overline{)12}$

$5\overline{)15}$ $5\overline{)5}$ $4\overline{)24}$ $4\overline{)32}$ $4\overline{)4}$

STOP   Time: _____ Number Completed: _____ Number Right: _____

6$\overline{)12}$ 7$\overline{)56}$ 8$\overline{)0}$ 8$\overline{)8}$

8$\overline{)40}$ 6$\overline{)54}$ 9$\overline{)45}$ 6$\overline{)48}$

7$\overline{)35}$ 7$\overline{)0}$ 6$\overline{)36}$ 9$\overline{)36}$

6$\overline{)42}$ 9$\overline{)18}$ 9$\overline{)27}$ 6$\overline{)18}$

9$\overline{)9}$ 6$\overline{)30}$ 7$\overline{)63}$ 6$\overline{)6}$

Time: _____   Number Completed: _____   Number Right: _____

$6\overline{)24}$ $7\overline{)28}$ $8\overline{)16}$ $8\overline{)72}$

$8\overline{)32}$ $9\overline{)72}$ $9\overline{)63}$ $7\overline{)42}$

$9\overline{)54}$ $8\overline{)56}$ $7\overline{)49}$ $8\overline{)64}$

$9\overline{)0}$ $7\overline{)7}$ $7\overline{)21}$ $8\overline{)24}$

$7\overline{)14}$ $8\overline{)48}$ $9\overline{)81}$ $6\overline{)12}$

Time: _____ Number Completed: _____ Number Right: _____

6)36   6)54   6)6   6)48

7)21   8)72   9)0   9)36

8)8   9)18   6)30   7)28

9)72   6)24   8)24   6)18

7)0   7)63   7)14   9)54

Time: _____   Number Completed: _____   Number Right: _____

$8\overline{)16}$ $\quad$ $7\overline{)7}$ $\quad$ $9\overline{)9}$ $\quad$ $9\overline{)54}$

$6\overline{)12}$ $\quad$ $9\overline{)27}$ $\quad$ $9\overline{)81}$ $\quad$ $8\overline{)64}$

$6\overline{)42}$ $\quad$ $6\overline{)48}$ $\quad$ $8\overline{)56}$ $\quad$ $7\overline{)14}$

$9\overline{)45}$ $\quad$ $9\overline{)63}$ $\quad$ $7\overline{)56}$ $\quad$ $8\overline{)32}$

$6\overline{)0}$ $\quad$ $7\overline{)35}$ $\quad$ $7\overline{)63}$ $\quad$ $7\overline{)49}$

STOP Time: _____ Number Completed: _____ Number Right: _____

$\qquad\qquad$ Just-a-Minute Math, SV 7940-5

$6\overline{)6}$ $9\overline{)45}$ $7\overline{)28}$ $6\overline{)0}$ $9\overline{)81}$

$8\overline{)24}$ $7\overline{)63}$ $6\overline{)42}$ $8\overline{)8}$ $6\overline{)36}$

$9\overline{)18}$ $9\overline{)72}$ $6\overline{)18}$ $8\overline{)56}$ $8\overline{)32}$

$7\overline{)49}$ $7\overline{)0}$ $7\overline{)14}$ $6\overline{)30}$ $9\overline{)36}$

$6\overline{)48}$ $9\overline{)54}$ $9\overline{)27}$ $9\overline{)0}$ $7\overline{)56}$

$6\overline{)54}$ $8\overline{)40}$ $8\overline{)64}$ $6\overline{)12}$ $8\overline{)48}$

Time: _____ Number Completed: _____ Number Right: _____

$8\overline{)72}$ $8\overline{)48}$ $7\overline{)63}$ $7\overline{)14}$ $9\overline{)0}$

$9\overline{)63}$ $9\overline{)9}$ $9\overline{)45}$ $8\overline{)40}$ $6\overline{)42}$

$7\overline{)35}$ $7\overline{)42}$ $6\overline{)0}$ $9\overline{)81}$ $9\overline{)27}$

$6\overline{)24}$ $8\overline{)16}$ $9\overline{)18}$ $6\overline{)18}$ $7\overline{)56}$

$8\overline{)0}$ $7\overline{)7}$ $8\overline{)32}$ $7\overline{)28}$ $6\overline{)36}$

$7\overline{)21}$ $6\overline{)54}$ $6\overline{)48}$ $9\overline{)36}$ $6\overline{)12}$

Time: _____ Number Completed: _____ Number Right: _____

Unit 4: Division/Facts for 6 Through 9
Just-a-Minute Math, SV 7940-5

$6\overline{)30}$ $6\overline{)48}$ $7\overline{)0}$ $8\overline{)8}$ $8\overline{)40}$

$6\overline{)6}$ $8\overline{)24}$ $8\overline{)72}$ $8\overline{)64}$ $6\overline{)12}$

$8\overline{)16}$ $7\overline{)7}$ $7\overline{)35}$ $9\overline{)36}$ $7\overline{)63}$

$9\overline{)9}$ $6\overline{)24}$ $7\overline{)49}$ $6\overline{)54}$ $9\overline{)45}$

$9\overline{)63}$ $9\overline{)72}$ $7\overline{)21}$ $7\overline{)14}$ $7\overline{)28}$

$9\overline{)54}$ $8\overline{)48}$ $7\overline{)42}$ $9\overline{)18}$ $6\overline{)0}$

Time: _____ Number Completed: _____ Number Right: _____

$6\overline{)6}$ $9\overline{)63}$ $9\overline{)72}$ $7\overline{)49}$ $8\overline{)56}$

$8\overline{)48}$ $7\overline{)56}$ $6\overline{)54}$ $6\overline{)48}$ $7\overline{)7}$

$7\overline{)42}$ $7\overline{)21}$ $6\overline{)18}$ $9\overline{)9}$ $6\overline{)0}$

$6\overline{)42}$ $8\overline{)32}$ $6\overline{)24}$ $8\overline{)24}$ $8\overline{)8}$

$7\overline{)0}$ $9\overline{)0}$ $9\overline{)54}$ $9\overline{)81}$ $8\overline{)64}$

$9\overline{)27}$ $6\overline{)36}$ $7\overline{)35}$ $6\overline{)30}$ $9\overline{)45}$

Time: _____ Number Completed: _____ Number Right: _____

Unit 4: Division/Facts for 6 Through 9
Just-a-Minute Math, SV 7940-5

$4\overline{)24}$ $7\overline{)35}$ $7\overline{)63}$ $3\overline{)12}$

$5\overline{)35}$ $8\overline{)48}$ $3\overline{)21}$ $1\overline{)6}$

$6\overline{)48}$ $4\overline{)36}$ $9\overline{)36}$ $3\overline{)27}$

$2\overline{)18}$ $2\overline{)8}$ $6\overline{)18}$ $4\overline{)12}$

$5\overline{)0}$ $5\overline{)5}$ $1\overline{)0}$ $9\overline{)0}$

Time: _____   Number Completed: _____   Number Right: _____

2)2   9)18   1)7   5)15

1)9   7)56   2)12   7)14

5)25   5)45   4)16   9)81

7)21   3)18   7)49   2)14

8)16   9)63   3)15   3)0

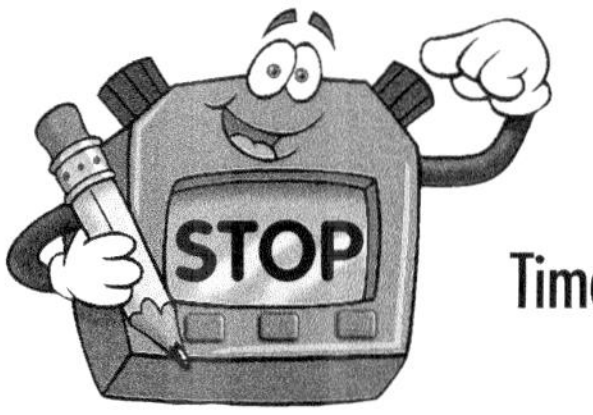

STOP   Time: _____ Number Completed: _____ Number Right: _____

6⟌36   9⟌9   4⟌0   8⟌64

8⟌32   7⟌42   2⟌10   9⟌27

1⟌8   5⟌40   3⟌3   8⟌72

3⟌24   2⟌4   5⟌30   5⟌20

2⟌16   3⟌6   7⟌28   2⟌6

Time: _____   Number Completed: _____   Number Right: _____

$6\overline{)6}$　　　　$6\overline{)30}$　　　　$3\overline{)9}$　　　　$6\overline{)42}$

$8\overline{)56}$　　　　$8\overline{)40}$　　　　$6\overline{)0}$　　　　$7\overline{)7}$

$9\overline{)45}$　　　　$9\overline{)72}$　　　　$4\overline{)28}$　　　　$8\overline{)24}$

$4\overline{)32}$　　　　$6\overline{)24}$　　　　$5\overline{)10}$　　　　$9\overline{)54}$

$2\overline{)0}$　　　　$5\overline{)0}$　　　　$6\overline{)12}$　　　　$4\overline{)20}$

STOP　Time: _____ Number Completed: _____ Number Right: _____

138

$1\overline{)1}$ $1\overline{)7}$ $8\overline{)16}$ $8\overline{)48}$ $5\overline{)20}$

$3\overline{)18}$ $2\overline{)0}$ $3\overline{)9}$ $3\overline{)24}$ $1\overline{)9}$

$7\overline{)35}$ $4\overline{)16}$ $9\overline{)54}$ $9\overline{)45}$ $7\overline{)56}$

$9\overline{)18}$ $6\overline{)36}$ $2\overline{)16}$ $7\overline{)14}$ $5\overline{)0}$

$4\overline{)36}$ $2\overline{)12}$ $8\overline{)0}$ $6\overline{)54}$ $3\overline{)12}$

$5\overline{)10}$ $2\overline{)0}$ $5\overline{)35}$ $2\overline{)2}$ $8\overline{)32}$

Time: _____ Number Completed: _____ Number Right: _____

Unit 4: Division/Mixed Facts for 1 Through 9
Just-a-Minute Math, SV 7940-5

$2\overline{)8}$	$5\overline{)45}$	$3\overline{)21}$	$5\overline{)25}$	$5\overline{)5}$
$4\overline{)12}$	$2\overline{)14}$	$6\overline{)48}$	$3\overline{)27}$	$6\overline{)6}$
$6\overline{)18}$	$7\overline{)21}$	$4\overline{)0}$	$2\overline{)18}$	$3\overline{)15}$
$9\overline{)9}$	$1\overline{)4}$	$6\overline{)42}$	$1\overline{)3}$	$7\overline{)28}$
$4\overline{)20}$	$7\overline{)42}$	$1\overline{)0}$	$6\overline{)24}$	$2\overline{)10}$
$9\overline{)72}$	$5\overline{)40}$	$9\overline{)27}$	$9\overline{)63}$	$6\overline{)0}$

Time: _____ Number Completed: _____ Number Right: _____

Unit 4: Division/Mixed Facts for 1 Through 9
Just-a-Minute Math, SV 7940-5

$1\overline{)2}$ $7\overline{)49}$ $5\overline{)15}$ $2\overline{)6}$ $8\overline{)24}$

$7\overline{)63}$ $9\overline{)81}$ $3\overline{)3}$ $4\overline{)0}$ $4\overline{)4}$

$5\overline{)30}$ $1\overline{)0}$ $5\overline{)0}$ $8\overline{)72}$ $8\overline{)8}$

$3\overline{)0}$ $3\overline{)6}$ $8\overline{)64}$ $4\overline{)8}$ $1\overline{)8}$

$8\overline{)56}$ $8\overline{)40}$ $6\overline{)12}$ $2\overline{)4}$ $7\overline{)42}$

$4\overline{)28}$ $9\overline{)36}$ $4\overline{)24}$ $6\overline{)30}$ $9\overline{)45}$

STOP

Time: _____   Number Completed: _____   Number Right: _____

$1\overline{)6}$ $\qquad$ $4\overline{)24}$ $\qquad$ $5\overline{)25}$ $\qquad$ $4\overline{)32}$ $\qquad$ $7\overline{)28}$

$3\overline{)18}$ $\qquad$ $2\overline{)16}$ $\qquad$ $9\overline{)81}$ $\qquad$ $2\overline{)12}$ $\qquad$ $1\overline{)10}$

$5\overline{)35}$ $\qquad$ $9\overline{)63}$ $\qquad$ $3\overline{)24}$ $\qquad$ $6\overline{)0}$ $\qquad$ $4\overline{)16}$

$9\overline{)54}$ $\qquad$ $5\overline{)0}$ $\qquad$ $7\overline{)7}$ $\qquad$ $2\overline{)4}$ $\qquad$ $8\overline{)64}$

$6\overline{)36}$ $\qquad$ $3\overline{)0}$ $\qquad$ $7\overline{)14}$ $\qquad$ $6\overline{)18}$ $\qquad$ $9\overline{)18}$

$5\overline{)45}$ $\qquad$ $6\overline{)24}$ $\qquad$ $9\overline{)27}$ $\qquad$ $8\overline{)56}$ $\qquad$ $3\overline{)15}$

Time: _____ Number Completed: _____ Number Right: _____

Unit 4: Division/Mixed Facts for 1 Through 9
Just-a-Minute Math, SV 7940-5

$3\overline{)12}$ $\qquad$ $6\overline{)30}$ $\qquad$ $4\overline{)20}$ $\qquad$ $7\overline{)49}$ $\qquad$ $8\overline{)48}$

$6\overline{)48}$ $\qquad$ $7\overline{)63}$ $\qquad$ $8\overline{)32}$ $\qquad$ $3\overline{)27}$ $\qquad$ $6\overline{)42}$

$9\overline{)36}$ $\qquad$ $2\overline{)8}$ $\qquad$ $7\overline{)35}$ $\qquad$ $8\overline{)72}$ $\qquad$ $4\overline{)8}$

$4\overline{)36}$ $\qquad$ $1\overline{)7}$ $\qquad$ $5\overline{)20}$ $\qquad$ $6\overline{)54}$ $\qquad$ $2\overline{)2}$

$2\overline{)0}$ $\qquad$ $6\overline{)12}$ $\qquad$ $3\overline{)9}$ $\qquad$ $5\overline{)15}$ $\qquad$ $1\overline{)0}$

$3\overline{)21}$ $\qquad$ $8\overline{)16}$ $\qquad$ $7\overline{)56}$ $\qquad$ $9\overline{)0}$ $\qquad$ $8\overline{)40}$

$9\overline{)9}$ $\qquad$ $9\overline{)72}$ $\qquad$ $8\overline{)8}$ $\qquad$ $4\overline{)0}$ $\qquad$ $8\overline{)24}$

$2\overline{)18}$ $\qquad$ $5\overline{)0}$ $\qquad$ $3\overline{)6}$ $\qquad$ $7\overline{)21}$ $\qquad$ $5\overline{)40}$

Time: _____ Number Completed: _____ Number Right: _____

Unit 4: Division/Mixed Facts for 1 Through 9
Just-a-Minute Math, SV 7940-5

$1\overline{)5}$ $4\overline{)16}$ $8\overline{)40}$ $3\overline{)24}$ $8\overline{)16}$

$5\overline{)30}$ $5\overline{)10}$ $9\overline{)18}$ $8\overline{)48}$ $3\overline{)18}$

$7\overline{)35}$ $1\overline{)9}$ $5\overline{)20}$ $2\overline{)16}$ $2\overline{)10}$

$9\overline{)72}$ $7\overline{)56}$ $7\overline{)63}$ $1\overline{)0}$ $8\overline{)56}$

$3\overline{)27}$ $9\overline{)54}$ $9\overline{)36}$ $6\overline{)42}$ $9\overline{)27}$

$3\overline{)0}$ $4\overline{)28}$ $4\overline{)32}$ $5\overline{)35}$ $2\overline{)8}$

$5\overline{)45}$ $3\overline{)15}$ $6\overline{)36}$ $9\overline{)81}$ $6\overline{)48}$

$9\overline{)63}$ $4\overline{)36}$ $9\overline{)45}$ $5\overline{)25}$ $2\overline{)18}$

Time: _____   Number Completed: _____   Number Right: _____

Unit 4: Division/Mixed Facts for 1 Through 9
Just-a-Minute Math, SV 7940-5

$6\overline{)18}$ $\qquad$ $4\overline{)12}$ $\qquad$ $9\overline{)0}$ $\qquad$ $6\overline{)0}$ $\qquad$ $2\overline{)0}$

$8\overline{)32}$ $\qquad$ $7\overline{)0}$ $\qquad$ $5\overline{)15}$ $\qquad$ $8\overline{)0}$ $\qquad$ $9\overline{)63}$

$9\overline{)9}$ $\qquad$ $1\overline{)8}$ $\qquad$ $6\overline{)12}$ $\qquad$ $6\overline{)54}$ $\qquad$ $8\overline{)56}$

$3\overline{)0}$ $\qquad$ $7\overline{)14}$ $\qquad$ $7\overline{)42}$ $\qquad$ $4\overline{)20}$ $\qquad$ $3\overline{)21}$

$2\overline{)12}$ $\qquad$ $5\overline{)30}$ $\qquad$ $8\overline{)24}$ $\qquad$ $2\overline{)10}$ $\qquad$ $9\overline{)45}$

$9\overline{)54}$ $\qquad$ $8\overline{)72}$ $\qquad$ $5\overline{)10}$ $\qquad$ $7\overline{)28}$ $\qquad$ $5\overline{)5}$

$8\overline{)64}$ $\qquad$ $5\overline{)40}$ $\qquad$ $3\overline{)12}$ $\qquad$ $2\overline{)8}$ $\qquad$ $3\overline{)9}$

$6\overline{)30}$ $\qquad$ $2\overline{)14}$ $\qquad$ $7\overline{)21}$ $\qquad$ $9\overline{)27}$ $\qquad$ $7\overline{)49}$

Time: _____ Number Completed: _____ Number Right: _____

6)24   5)45   6)18   2)0   5)0

9)36   2)2   4)12   2)18   2)10

5)35   1)9   9)18   6)12   9)27

9)81   6)0   3)15   3)18   5)15

3)27   9)72   9)54   5)25   7)49

5)30   5)20   4)36   9)63   6)42

9)45   4)28   6)30   6)54   9)36

6)48   8)40   2)14   5)40   4)24

Time: _____   Number Completed: _____   Number Right: _____

www.harcourtschoolsupply.com
© Harcourt Achieve Inc. All rights reserved.

Unit 4: Division/Mixed Facts for 1 Through 9
Just-a-Minute Math, SV 7940-5

$6\overline{)42}$ $6\overline{)18}$ $4\overline{)24}$ $9\overline{)54}$ $5\overline{)35}$

$4\overline{)32}$ $9\overline{)63}$ $2\overline{)2}$ $6\overline{)54}$ $6\overline{)24}$

$2\overline{)16}$ $5\overline{)0}$ $7\overline{)63}$ $6\overline{)36}$ $8\overline{)40}$

$6\overline{)36}$ $4\overline{)0}$ $7\overline{)7}$ $3\overline{)15}$ $1\overline{)9}$

$8\overline{)48}$ $5\overline{)15}$ $3\overline{)9}$ $1\overline{)3}$ $4\overline{)0}$

$7\overline{)56}$ $4\overline{)16}$ $3\overline{)24}$ $8\overline{)64}$ $9\overline{)45}$

$5\overline{)30}$ $9\overline{)18}$ $7\overline{)21}$ $7\overline{)28}$ $8\overline{)16}$

$8\overline{)24}$ $3\overline{)27}$ $2\overline{)0}$ $4\overline{)28}$ $4\overline{)8}$

$3\overline{)18}$ $7\overline{)35}$ $1\overline{)7}$ $5\overline{)40}$ $3\overline{)21}$

$2\overline{)8}$ $6\overline{)30}$ $7\overline{)49}$ $4\overline{)20}$ $7\overline{)42}$

STOP   Time: _____   Number Completed: _____   Number Right: _____

Unit 4: Division/Mixed Facts for 1 Through 9
Just-a-Minute Math, SV 7940-5

$6\overline{)0}$ $5\overline{)20}$ $5\overline{)10}$ $3\overline{)18}$ $7\overline{)35}$

$5\overline{)45}$ $3\overline{)21}$ $8\overline{)8}$ $5\overline{)30}$ $8\overline{)40}$

$6\overline{)12}$ $2\overline{)14}$ $4\overline{)36}$ $6\overline{)24}$ $9\overline{)54}$

$8\overline{)56}$ $1\overline{)8}$ $2\overline{)10}$ $3\overline{)27}$ $3\overline{)21}$

$4\overline{)20}$ $9\overline{)27}$ $4\overline{)12}$ $8\overline{)72}$ $2\overline{)4}$

$3\overline{)6}$ $9\overline{)9}$ $1\overline{)5}$ $9\overline{)36}$ $7\overline{)42}$

$2\overline{)18}$ $6\overline{)48}$ $6\overline{)30}$ $9\overline{)18}$ $6\overline{)36}$

$9\overline{)72}$ $2\overline{)6}$ $7\overline{)21}$ $7\overline{)7}$ $3\overline{)24}$

$8\overline{)32}$ $5\overline{)25}$ $9\overline{)45}$ $4\overline{)28}$ $2\overline{)16}$

$7\overline{)14}$ $9\overline{)81}$ $7\overline{)56}$ $4\overline{)8}$ $7\overline{)49}$

STOP   Time: _____   Number Completed: _____   Number Right: _____

$5\overline{)35}$ $8\overline{)24}$ $3\overline{)15}$ $9\overline{)81}$ $3\overline{)6}$

$6\overline{)24}$ $7\overline{)28}$ $2\overline{)10}$ $5\overline{)25}$ $4\overline{)32}$

$2\overline{)14}$ $5\overline{)20}$ $1\overline{)7}$ $6\overline{)0}$ $8\overline{)56}$

$5\overline{)10}$ $9\overline{)63}$ $6\overline{)54}$ $4\overline{)16}$ $9\overline{)27}$

$7\overline{)0}$ $2\overline{)18}$ $8\overline{)8}$ $5\overline{)15}$ $5\overline{)5}$

$9\overline{)9}$ $6\overline{)12}$ $9\overline{)72}$ $3\overline{)21}$ $3\overline{)3}$

$2\overline{)12}$ $6\overline{)48}$ $7\overline{)63}$ $9\overline{)36}$ $8\overline{)32}$

$2\overline{)6}$ $5\overline{)40}$ $5\overline{)45}$ $8\overline{)48}$ $8\overline{)72}$

$6\overline{)18}$ $4\overline{)20}$ $3\overline{)9}$ $8\overline{)64}$ $2\overline{)4}$

$7\overline{)14}$ $2\overline{)8}$ $8\overline{)16}$ $5\overline{)30}$ $4\overline{)36}$

STOP   Time: _____   Number Completed: _____   Number Right: _____

9)18	7)21	2)6	9)27	3)21
5)20	9)45	4)12	5)30	7)7
6)36	7)35	5)40	6)54	8)24
8)40	3)18	4)8	8)56	9)36
2)16	2)2	9)45	3)0	6)48
6)30	3)24	5)25	1)0	5)45
2)14	6)24	1)5	9)9	3)27
5)5	9)72	6)24	7)49	2)10
7)56	7)63	7)14	3)9	2)18
4)24	6)18	8)16	5)10	7)28

STOP

Time: _____ Number Completed: _____ Number Right: _____

Unit 4: Division/Mixed Facts for 1 Through 9
Just-a-Minute Math, SV 7940-5

Name _____ Date _____ **Division Test No. 33** *(60)*

5)15	6)24	5)25	7)0	6)42	6)54
2)0	5)40	9)54	4)16	9)63	4)32
7)56	4)36	2)14	6)36	2)6	3)21
6)48	2)10	8)40	7)42	8)8	2)12
3)27	1)10	5)0	9)18	6)30	1)0
9)72	9)36	2)18	6)0	9)27	8)64
3)0	4)20	5)35	9)45	4)24	6)18
3)18	3)3	3)24	7)49	7)35	5)45
7)28	3)9	8)48	4)28	2)16	4)12
8)56	8)24	9)81	1)7	9)9	3)15

Time: _____ Number Completed: _____ Number Right: _____

$5\overline{)20}$ $9\overline{)45}$ $5\overline{)25}$ $7\overline{)35}$ $4\overline{)8}$ $9\overline{)9}$

$8\overline{)72}$ $3\overline{)27}$ $7\overline{)42}$ $9\overline{)72}$ $9\overline{)36}$ $6\overline{)48}$

$7\overline{)63}$ $2\overline{)8}$ $8\overline{)48}$ $4\overline{)16}$ $3\overline{)24}$ $5\overline{)5}$

$6\overline{)12}$ $8\overline{)16}$ $4\overline{)32}$ $2\overline{)14}$ $7\overline{)56}$ $6\overline{)18}$

$5\overline{)30}$ $2\overline{)2}$ $1\overline{)0}$ $7\overline{)21}$ $6\overline{)42}$ $1\overline{)3}$

$4\overline{)0}$ $5\overline{)35}$ $7\overline{)49}$ $2\overline{)0}$ $7\overline{)28}$ $4\overline{)24}$

$3\overline{)12}$ $8\overline{)56}$ $9\overline{)27}$ $3\overline{)18}$ $9\overline{)81}$ $7\overline{)14}$

$8\overline{)32}$ $5\overline{)0}$ $5\overline{)45}$ $9\overline{)54}$ $4\overline{)28}$ $6\overline{)36}$

$7\overline{)7}$ $8\overline{)64}$ $3\overline{)21}$ $6\overline{)0}$ $6\overline{)30}$ $5\overline{)40}$

$3\overline{)6}$ $9\overline{)63}$ $2\overline{)16}$ $4\overline{)20}$ $8\overline{)24}$ $6\overline{)54}$

STOP   Time: _____   Number Completed: _____   Number Right: _____

Unit 4: Division/Mixed Facts for 1 Through 9
Just-a-Minute Math, SV 7940-5

$2\overline{)4}$ $2\overline{)0}$ $4\overline{)36}$ $8\overline{)32}$ $2\overline{)12}$ $8\overline{)24}$

$6\overline{)24}$ $8\overline{)8}$ $7\overline{)14}$ $7\overline{)42}$ $8\overline{)56}$ $7\overline{)21}$

$1\overline{)8}$ $6\overline{)54}$ $9\overline{)18}$ $5\overline{)35}$ $9\overline{)54}$ $5\overline{)25}$

$7\overline{)63}$ $4\overline{)32}$ $8\overline{)64}$ $4\overline{)16}$ $4\overline{)24}$ $3\overline{)24}$

$3\overline{)9}$ $9\overline{)27}$ $8\overline{)72}$ $8\overline{)40}$ $3\overline{)18}$ $9\overline{)0}$

$7\overline{)35}$ $3\overline{)15}$ $5\overline{)45}$ $9\overline{)72}$ $7\overline{)56}$ $4\overline{)8}$

$8\overline{)48}$ $5\overline{)15}$ $2\overline{)10}$ $3\overline{)27}$ $9\overline{)36}$ $6\overline{)18}$

$9\overline{)45}$ $9\overline{)63}$ $7\overline{)0}$ $5\overline{)10}$ $2\overline{)6}$ $7\overline{)49}$

$6\overline{)48}$ $2\overline{)18}$ $6\overline{)12}$ $8\overline{)0}$ $6\overline{)36}$ $3\overline{)21}$

$4\overline{)12}$ $5\overline{)20}$ $4\overline{)28}$ $5\overline{)40}$ $9\overline{)81}$ $7\overline{)28}$

Time: _____ Number Completed: _____ Number Right: _____

Just-a-Minute Math, SV 7940-5

$4\overline{)20}$ $8\overline{)32}$ $1\overline{)9}$ $2\overline{)18}$ $2\overline{)16}$ $6\overline{)42}$

$8\overline{)0}$ $4\overline{)36}$ $4\overline{)28}$ $8\overline{)64}$ $9\overline{)18}$ $5\overline{)20}$

$5\overline{)35}$ $6\overline{)54}$ $8\overline{)16}$ $9\overline{)45}$ $6\overline{)24}$ $4\overline{)24}$

$9\overline{)54}$ $9\overline{)81}$ $5\overline{)45}$ $3\overline{)15}$ $5\overline{)25}$ $3\overline{)0}$

$2\overline{)14}$ $3\overline{)27}$ $7\overline{)63}$ $2\overline{)2}$ $4\overline{)32}$ $5\overline{)15}$

$2\overline{)0}$ $6\overline{)36}$ $8\overline{)48}$ $9\overline{)36}$ $8\overline{)40}$ $8\overline{)24}$

$8\overline{)0}$ $9\overline{)27}$ $5\overline{)30}$ $6\overline{)48}$ $3\overline{)18}$ $7\overline{)21}$

$3\overline{)9}$ $7\overline{)42}$ $2\overline{)8}$ $4\overline{)12}$ $9\overline{)72}$ $6\overline{)30}$

$6\overline{)18}$ $7\overline{)28}$ $5\overline{)0}$ $7\overline{)49}$ $8\overline{)56}$ $4\overline{)16}$

$5\overline{)10}$ $3\overline{)21}$ $9\overline{)63}$ $3\overline{)24}$ $7\overline{)35}$ $7\overline{)56}$

STOP   Time: _____   Number Completed: _____   Number Right: _____

```
   2            9            3
 + 3          - 3          x 6          6)36
```

```
   8            4                         3
 - 5          x 2         8)40          + 5
```

```
   3                         5            6
 x 4          3)6          + 7          - 4
```

```
                1           13            0
7)28          + 3          - 8          x 1
```

```
   7            7            1
 + 6          - 2          x 7          2)4
```

Time: _____ Number Completed: _____ Number Right: _____

155
Unit 5: Mixed Facts
Just-a-Minute Math, SV 7940-5

$$\begin{array}{r} 9 \\ + 5 \\ \hline \end{array}\qquad \begin{array}{r} 8 \\ - 7 \\ \hline \end{array}\qquad \begin{array}{r} 6 \\ \times 5 \\ \hline \end{array}\qquad 6\overline{)24}$$

$$\begin{array}{r} 8 \\ - 8 \\ \hline \end{array}\qquad \begin{array}{r} 1 \\ \times 3 \\ \hline \end{array}\qquad 8\overline{)56}\qquad \begin{array}{r} 4 \\ + 8 \\ \hline \end{array}$$

$$\begin{array}{r} 5 \\ \times 9 \\ \hline \end{array}\qquad 2\overline{)10}\qquad \begin{array}{r} 6 \\ + 9 \\ \hline \end{array}\qquad \begin{array}{r} 12 \\ - 7 \\ \hline \end{array}$$

$$9\overline{)18}\qquad \begin{array}{r} 2 \\ + 4 \\ \hline \end{array}\qquad \begin{array}{r} 7 \\ - 3 \\ \hline \end{array}\qquad \begin{array}{r} 6 \\ \times 6 \\ \hline \end{array}$$

$$\begin{array}{r} 7 \\ + 8 \\ \hline \end{array}\qquad \begin{array}{r} 7 \\ - 6 \\ \hline \end{array}\qquad \begin{array}{r} 7 \\ \times 8 \\ \hline \end{array}\qquad 3\overline{)21}$$

Time: _____ Number Completed: _____ Number Right: _____

Unit 5: Mixed Facts
Just-a-Minute Math, SV 7940-5

$$\begin{array}{r} 8 \\ +\ 7 \\ \hline \end{array} \qquad \begin{array}{r} 5 \\ -\ 5 \\ \hline \end{array} \qquad \begin{array}{r} 4 \\ \times\ 1 \\ \hline \end{array} \qquad 3\overline{)\,0\ \ }$$

$$\begin{array}{r} 15 \\ -\ 7 \\ \hline \end{array} \qquad \begin{array}{r} 2 \\ \times\ 8 \\ \hline \end{array} \qquad 8\overline{)\,16\ } \qquad \begin{array}{r} 5 \\ +\ 5 \\ \hline \end{array}$$

$$\begin{array}{r} 5 \\ \times\ 3 \\ \hline \end{array} \qquad 9\overline{)\,36\ } \qquad \begin{array}{r} 3 \\ +\ 6 \\ \hline \end{array} \qquad \begin{array}{r} 11 \\ -\ 4 \\ \hline \end{array}$$

$$3\overline{)\,15\ } \qquad \begin{array}{r} 2 \\ +\ 2 \\ \hline \end{array} \qquad \begin{array}{r} 11 \\ -\ 5 \\ \hline \end{array} \qquad \begin{array}{r} 9 \\ \times\ 8 \\ \hline \end{array}$$

$$\begin{array}{r} 6 \\ +\ 5 \\ \hline \end{array} \qquad \begin{array}{r} 4 \\ -\ 1 \\ \hline \end{array} \qquad \begin{array}{r} 4 \\ \times\ 5 \\ \hline \end{array} \qquad 3\overline{)\,18\ }$$

Time: _____ Number Completed: _____ Number Right: _____

0 + 0	3 − 2	4)20̄	8 + 3
7 − 5	7 x 4	7 + 4	13 − 6
2 x 6	5)20̄	9 − 5	2 x 4
1)8̄	8 + 5	9 x 6	1)4̄
4 + 4	13 − 9	9)63̄	2 + 8

Time: _____   Number Completed: _____   Number Right: _____

```
    4           3           5           2           5
  + 3         x 7         + 9         x 5         + 6


   11                      10                      13
  - 6        7)7          - 9        9)54         - 7


    3           5           4           0           6
  x 5         + 2         x 3         + 2         x 4


              12                      11
  7)14        - 8        4)16         - 9        4)28


    7           5           1           9           7
  + 5         x 6         + 5         x 5         + 3


    6                       4                      15
  - 5        8)24         - 3        7)35         - 9
```

Time: _____   Number Completed: _____   Number Right: _____

Unit 5: Mixed Facts
Just-a-Minute Math, SV 7940-5

1 x 6	5 + 8	6 x 7	6 + 6	9 x 3

5)35	14 − 7	4)32	7 − 4	7)42

3 + 4	5 x 8	3 + 3	4 x 8	6 + 4

8 − 6	3)12	9 − 6	2)2	15 − 6

6 x 2	6 + 3	5 x 4	1 + 1	7 x 1

6)42	8 − 3	8)32	9 − 4	4)8

Time: _____ Number Completed: _____ Number Right: _____

```
  2          8          2          3          7
+ 5        x 9        + 6        x 3        + 7
```

```
  7                    10                    10
- 7      3)24         - 8      4)12         - 6
```

```
  2          9          6          3          1
x 2        + 4        x 9        + 7        x 4
```

```
2)16         9        3)27        6        4)24
           - 0                  - 3
```

```
  6          9          4          0          6
+ 7        x 4        + 5        x 6        + 8
```

```
 12                     5                    12
- 3      1)9          - 2      5)15         - 6
```

Time: _____   Number Completed: _____   Number Right: _____

Name _____ Date _____ *Mixed Facts Test No. 8* *(30)*

$$\begin{array}{r} 4 \\ \times\,9 \\ \hline \end{array}$$ $$\begin{array}{r} 8 \\ +\,6 \\ \hline \end{array}$$ $$\begin{array}{r} 1 \\ \times\,8 \\ \hline \end{array}$$ $$\begin{array}{r} 4 \\ +\,7 \\ \hline \end{array}$$ $$\begin{array}{r} 7 \\ \times\,2 \\ \hline \end{array}$$

$6\,)\overline{30}$ $$\begin{array}{r} 14 \\ -\,5 \\ \hline \end{array}$$ $6\,)\overline{12}$ $$\begin{array}{r} 6 \\ -\,6 \\ \hline \end{array}$$ $5\,)\overline{30}$

$$\begin{array}{r} 9 \\ +\,6 \\ \hline \end{array}$$ $$\begin{array}{r} 5 \\ \times\,7 \\ \hline \end{array}$$ $$\begin{array}{r} 8 \\ +\,8 \\ \hline \end{array}$$ $$\begin{array}{r} 0 \\ \times\,4 \\ \hline \end{array}$$ $$\begin{array}{r} 8 \\ +\,4 \\ \hline \end{array}$$

$$\begin{array}{r} 5 \\ -\,4 \\ \hline \end{array}$$ $2\,)\overline{14}$ $$\begin{array}{r} 8 \\ -\,4 \\ \hline \end{array}$$ $4\,)\overline{0}$ $$\begin{array}{r} 10 \\ -\,7 \\ \hline \end{array}$$

$$\begin{array}{r} 0 \\ \times\,0 \\ \hline \end{array}$$ $$\begin{array}{r} 7 \\ +\,2 \\ \hline \end{array}$$ $$\begin{array}{r} 4 \\ \times\,7 \\ \hline \end{array}$$ $$\begin{array}{r} 4 \\ +\,9 \\ \hline \end{array}$$ $$\begin{array}{r} 0 \\ \times\,5 \\ \hline \end{array}$$

$9\,)\overline{27}$ $$\begin{array}{r} 14 \\ -\,8 \\ \hline \end{array}$$ $6\,)\overline{18}$ $$\begin{array}{r} 17 \\ -\,8 \\ \hline \end{array}$$ $7\,)\overline{56}$

Time: _____ Number Completed: _____ Number Right: _____

162

Unit 5: Mixed Facts
Just-a-Minute Math, SV 7940-5

0 + 9	4 + 6	5 + 3	7 + 9	7 + 0
16 − 7	14 − 9	2 − 0	15 − 8	12 − 5
4 x 6	7 x 9	8 x 7	0 x 9	6 x 8
8⟌64	9⟌81	5⟌5	1⟌1	9⟌45
9 + 7	0 + 4	5 + 4	3 + 8	0 + 7
11 − 8	2 − 1	13 − 4	11 − 7	7 − 1
4 x 4	7 x 6	8 x 8	9 x 7	5 x 5
3⟌9	5⟌40	6⟌54	6⟌48	7⟌49

Time: _____ Number Completed: _____ Number Right: _____

```
    0          2          3          9          9
  + 5        + 9        + 9        + 8        + 3
```

```
    4          9         13         14         11
  - 4        - 7        - 5        - 6        - 3
```

```
    6          0          3          5          7
  x 3        x 3        x 9        x 2        x 5
```

```
8)72       9)9        5)45       4)36       2)18
```

```
    9          4          8          2          3
  + 9        + 2        + 9        + 7        + 2
```

```
   16          5          9         12         10
  - 8        - 3        - 8        - 9        - 5
```

```
    8          3          0          8          2
  x 5        x 8        x 7        x 4        x 9
```

```
5)25       2)12       2)6        5)10       8)48
```

Time: _____ Number Completed: _____ Number Right: _____

Just-a-Minute Math, SV 7940-5

$$9 + 2$$ $$6 + 2$$ $$10 - 3$$ $$10 - 4$$ $$18 - 9$$

$$9 - 9$$ $$17 - 9$$ $$4 \times 0$$ $$9 \times 2$$ $$2 \times 7$$

$$8 \times 3$$ $$7 \times 7$$ $$8\overline{)0}$$ $$3\overline{)3}$$ $$6\overline{)0}$$

$$2\overline{)8}$$ $$8 + 2$$ $$1 + 7$$ $$1 + 4$$ $$3 + 8$$

$$4 + 1$$ $$16 - 9$$ $$12 - 4$$ $$6 - 2$$ $$11 - 2$$

$$10 - 1$$ $$1 \times 1$$ $$2 \times 3$$ $$1 \times 9$$ $$7 \times 3$$

$$1 \times 5$$ $$7\overline{)63}$$ $$2\overline{)0}$$ $$7\overline{)21}$$ $$1\overline{)6}$$

$$9\overline{)72}$$ $$5 + 0$$ $$1 + 8$$ $$0 + 6$$ $$6 + 7$$

Time: _____ Number Completed: _____ Number Right: _____

Just-a-Minute Math, SV 7940-5

7	6	1	4	3
+ 7	+ 8	+ 5	+ 4	+ 4

8	12	8	14	16
− 3	− 7	− 5	− 8	− 7

5	7	5	3	5
x 4	x 4	x 5	x 7	x 8

5⟌35	3⟌6	9⟌63	3⟌9	8⟌56

2	4	7	5	7
+ 6	+ 5	+ 9	+ 8	+ 5

9	9	13	12	7
− 5	− 6	− 9	− 6	− 6

6	6	2	0	5
x 6	x 7	+ 6	x 6	x 6

5⟌15	6⟌42	7⟌49	3⟌18	8⟌40

STOP

Time: _____ Number Completed: _____ Number Right: _____

3 + 7	0 x 2	6 + 5	8)16	14 − 7
11 − 8	6)12	8 − 4	7 + 8	8 x 2
3 x 4	5 + 9	6 x 5	3 − 1	7)42
4)12	6 − 4	4)28	7 x 2	1 + 6
4 + 9	4 x 4	6 + 6	9)81	5 − 0
6 − 6	8)48	12 − 5	2 + 8	9 x 5
4 x 7	5 + 3	6 x 3	11 − 9	3)21
4)20	4 − 2	5)30	3 x 6	8 + 8
4 + 3	2 x 5	9 + 5	2)10	15 − 8
3 − 3	3)12	7 − 5	8 + 5	6 x 8

Time: _____   **Number Completed:** _____   **Number Right:** _____

167
Unit 5: Mixed Facts
Just-a-Minute Math, SV 7940-5

$8 \overline{)64}$

$\begin{array}{r} 6 \\ -5 \\ \hline \end{array}$

$1 \overline{)8}$

$\begin{array}{r} 14 \\ -5 \\ \hline \end{array}$

$4 \overline{)32}$

$\begin{array}{r} 4 \\ +8 \\ \hline \end{array}$

$\begin{array}{r} 6 \\ \times 4 \\ \hline \end{array}$

$\begin{array}{r} 9 \\ +7 \\ \hline \end{array}$

$\begin{array}{r} 4 \\ \times 6 \\ \hline \end{array}$

$\begin{array}{r} 8 \\ +3 \\ \hline \end{array}$

$\begin{array}{r} 13 \\ -8 \\ \hline \end{array}$

$7 \overline{)35}$

$\begin{array}{r} 17 \\ -8 \\ \hline \end{array}$

$9 \overline{)45}$

$\begin{array}{r} 8 \\ -7 \\ \hline \end{array}$

$\begin{array}{r} 7 \\ \times 8 \\ \hline \end{array}$

$\begin{array}{r} 7 \\ +2 \\ \hline \end{array}$

$\begin{array}{r} 9 \\ \times 8 \\ \hline \end{array}$

$\begin{array}{r} 5 \\ +4 \\ \hline \end{array}$

$\begin{array}{r} 6 \\ \times 0 \\ \hline \end{array}$

$8 \overline{)32}$

$\begin{array}{r} 11 \\ -7 \\ \hline \end{array}$

$9 \overline{)54}$

$\begin{array}{r} 15 \\ -9 \\ \hline \end{array}$

$4 \overline{)16}$

$\begin{array}{r} 3 \\ +5 \\ \hline \end{array}$

$\begin{array}{r} 8 \\ \times 8 \\ \hline \end{array}$

$\begin{array}{r} 5 \\ +7 \\ \hline \end{array}$

$\begin{array}{r} 2 \\ \times 4 \\ \hline \end{array}$

$\begin{array}{r} 5 \\ +5 \\ \hline \end{array}$

$\begin{array}{r} 7 \\ -4 \\ \hline \end{array}$

$6 \overline{)24}$

$\begin{array}{r} 11 \\ -6 \\ \hline \end{array}$

$6 \overline{)48}$

$\begin{array}{r} 9 \\ -3 \\ \hline \end{array}$

$\begin{array}{r} 3 \\ \times 2 \\ \hline \end{array}$

$\begin{array}{r} 0 \\ +1 \\ \hline \end{array}$

$\begin{array}{r} 5 \\ \times 7 \\ \hline \end{array}$

$\begin{array}{r} 8 \\ +4 \\ \hline \end{array}$

$\begin{array}{r} 8 \\ \times 6 \\ \hline \end{array}$

$9 \overline{)36}$

$\begin{array}{r} 4 \\ -0 \\ \hline \end{array}$

$9 \overline{)72}$

$\begin{array}{r} 7 \\ -3 \\ \hline \end{array}$

$4 \overline{)24}$

$\begin{array}{r} 8 \\ +7 \\ \hline \end{array}$

$\begin{array}{r} 9 \\ \times 3 \\ \hline \end{array}$

$\begin{array}{r} 6 \\ +9 \\ \hline \end{array}$

$\begin{array}{r} 7 \\ \times 6 \\ \hline \end{array}$

$\begin{array}{r} 2 \\ +4 \\ \hline \end{array}$

Time: _____ Number Completed: _____ Number Right: _____

Unit 5: Mixed Facts
Just-a-Minute Math, SV 7940-5

0 − 0	3⟌27	4 − 3	7⟌28	11 − 4
6 × 1	8 + 6	6 × 9	2 + 5	5 × 1
6⟌30	10 − 2	7⟌56	15 − 7	6⟌36
3 + 6	8 × 1	6 + 4	5 × 9	7 + 4
9 − 4	3⟌15	9 − 2	3⟌24	13 − 7
2 × 8	7 + 6	9 × 9	5 + 6	7 × 9
2⟌14	12 − 8	9⟌18	14 − 9	9⟌27
1 + 9	4 × 8	6 + 3	9 × 4	4 + 6
8 − 0	6⟌54	8 − 2	2⟌16	7 − 2
5 × 3	9 + 6	4 × 5	9 + 4	9 × 6

Time: _____ Number Completed: _____ Number Right: _____

Unit 5: Mixed Facts
Just-a-Minute Math, SV 7940-5

$7\overline{)14}$ 13 − 4 $8\overline{)72}$ 10 − 7 $5\overline{)20}$

7 + 3   1 × 6   9 + 3   2 × 2   5 + 2

8 − 6 $1\overline{)7}$ 15 − 6 $8\overline{)24}$ 8 − 1

3 × 5   9 + 8   3 × 3   2 + 7   7 × 5

$4\overline{)8}$ 13 − 6 $2\overline{)12}$ 2 − 2 $7\overline{)21}$

3 + 3   8 × 6   2 + 3   7 × 3   6 + 1

11 − 5 $5\overline{)40}$ 11 − 3 $4\overline{)36}$ 12 − 4

4 × 9   8 + 9   8 × 3   0 + 3   8 × 7

$3\overline{)0}$ 16 − 8 $2\overline{)8}$ 12 − 3 $4\overline{)4}$

4 + 7   7 × 7   3 + 9   1 × 7   9 + 9

STOP

Time: _____ Number Completed: _____ Number Right: _____

Unit 5: Mixed Facts
Just-a-Minute Math, SV 7940-5

17 − 9	2)6	13 − 5	1)3	6 − 0	8)56
8 × 9	2 + 9	9 × 9	7 + 8	7 × 4	4 + 4
5)45	14 − 6	6)6	1 − 1	6)24	10 − 4
6 + 2	9 × 7	3 + 5	9 × 0	4 + 0	9 × 3
18 − 9	6)18	6 − 3	7)49	6 − 1	3)27
0 × 8	8 + 2	3 × 9	9 + 7	3 × 4	7 + 9
2)18	9 − 9	5)10	17 − 8	6)42	11 − 2
1 + 8	6 × 2	5 + 9	8 × 5	5 + 7	2 × 3
6 − 2	7)63	13 − 8	7)0	14 − 5	8)8
1 × 5	9 + 2	2 × 0	6 + 9	6 × 7	4 + 9

Time: _____ Number Completed: _____ Number Right: _____

3 − 0	7)‾35‾	5 − 1	9)‾0‾	15 − 7	5)‾35‾
5 × 6	6 + 6	2 × 6	8 + 6	7 × 8	6 + 7
1)‾0‾	1 − 0	5)‾0‾	8 − 4	7)‾42‾	14 − 8
2 + 5	9 × 4	6 + 5	6 × 5	7 + 7	5 × 8
11 − 4	5)‾45‾	13 − 7	9)‾72‾	9 − 6	4)‾32‾
6 × 6	4 + 5	2 × 9	0 + 8	8 × 4	7 + 4
4)‾24‾	11 − 6	5)‾25‾	8 − 7	6)‾54‾	12 − 5
5 + 8	9 × 6	8 + 8	1 × 2	7 + 6	7 × 9
15 − 8	4)‾28‾	16 − 7	6)‾36‾	7 − 0	9)‾54‾
4 × 6	9 + 6	3 × 6	9 + 5	3 × 8	6 + 8

Time: _____ Number Completed: _____ Number Right: _____

Unit 5: Mixed Facts
Just-a-Minute Math, SV 7940-5

16 − 9	7)56	7 − 6	3)15	16 − 7	8)40

7 × 6	8 + 7	4 × 5	5 + 1	5 × 6	7 + 9

5)30	9 − 1	7)28	14 − 7	4)36	14 − 8

7 + 5	3 × 7	5 + 4	6 × 4	4 + 7	6 × 9

9 − 8	8)64	10 − 2	9)63	13 − 9	9)81

4 × 3	8 + 5	9 × 8	5 + 3	7 × 5	9 + 3

6)48	12 − 6	9)27	12 − 7	9)54	18 − 9

5 + 6	9 × 5	9 + 9	8 × 8	6 + 7	9 × 4

10 − 3	8)48	5 − 2	7)49	14 − 6	4)24

9 × 9	4 + 8	5 × 8	6 + 8	6 × 7	5 + 9

Time: _____ Number Completed: _____ Number Right: _____

```
  17                    10                   7
 - 8      6)30         - 6      2)18        - 3      9)54

   8        7            4        9           2        9
 x 7      + 6          x 6      + 5         x 8      + 4

          16                   13                    11
 5)40    - 8      4)12        - 4      5)15         - 7

   8        7            7        4           9        4
 + 6      x 8          + 7      x 8         + 6      x 4

  15                    13                   14
 - 9      9)72         - 7      3)21        - 5      2)14

   7        7            5        3           9        4
 x 3      + 4          x 5      + 4         x 6      + 4

          17                    9                    15
 9)45    - 9      4)20         - 3      7)63         - 7

   8        7            9        7           6        2
 + 8      x 7          + 8      x 2         + 6      x 9

  11                    15                   12
 - 4      6)42         - 6      2)8         - 5      3)24

   6        8            6        7           5        3
 x 5      + 9          x 6      + 2         x 7      + 6
```

Time: _____   Number Completed: _____   Number Right: _____

Unit 5: Mixed Facts
Just-a-Minute Math, SV 7940-5

$\frac{6}{8}$ ☐ $\frac{12}{12}$ ☐ $\frac{6}{36}$ ☐ $\frac{6}{18}$ ☐

$\frac{5}{10}$ ☐ $\frac{3}{6}$ ☐ $\frac{11}{33}$ ☐ $\frac{10}{10}$ ☐

$\frac{7}{28}$ ☐ $\frac{4}{28}$ ☐ $\frac{4}{40}$ ☐ $\frac{14}{21}$ ☐

$\frac{10}{25}$ ☐ $\frac{20}{30}$ ☐ $\frac{12}{36}$ ☐ $\frac{5}{25}$ ☐

$\frac{12}{18}$ ☐ $\frac{5}{30}$ ☐ $\frac{7}{14}$ ☐ $\frac{2}{12}$ ☐

STOP   Time: _____   Number Completed: _____   Number Right: _____

175   Unit 6: Fractions in Simplest Form/One or Less
Just-a-Minute Math, SV 7940-5

$\dfrac{8}{20}$ ☐ $\dfrac{8}{16}$ ☐ $\dfrac{14}{28}$ ☐ $\dfrac{15}{25}$ ☐

$\dfrac{9}{36}$ ☐ $\dfrac{9}{27}$ ☐ $\dfrac{12}{16}$ ☐ $\dfrac{18}{21}$ ☐

$\dfrac{5}{40}$ ☐ $\dfrac{20}{25}$ ☐ $\dfrac{8}{24}$ ☐ $\dfrac{2}{14}$ ☐

$\dfrac{4}{16}$ ☐ $\dfrac{9}{30}$ ☐ $\dfrac{16}{16}$ ☐ $\dfrac{20}{40}$ ☐

$\dfrac{3}{24}$ ☐ $\dfrac{2}{24}$ ☐ $\dfrac{8}{28}$ ☐ $\dfrac{12}{39}$ ☐

STOP

Time: _____   Number Completed: _____   Number Right: _____

$\dfrac{10}{40}$ ☐ $\dfrac{14}{18}$ ☐ $\dfrac{15}{33}$ ☐ $\dfrac{3}{9}$ ☐ $\dfrac{6}{16}$ ☐

$\dfrac{10}{18}$ ☐ $\dfrac{6}{9}$ ☐ $\dfrac{2}{28}$ ☐ $\dfrac{1}{1}$ ☐ $\dfrac{4}{8}$ ☐

$\dfrac{18}{24}$ ☐ $\dfrac{8}{12}$ ☐ $\dfrac{13}{26}$ ☐ $\dfrac{2}{8}$ ☐ $\dfrac{2}{16}$ ☐

$\dfrac{6}{30}$ ☐ $\dfrac{14}{14}$ ☐ $\dfrac{4}{14}$ ☐ $\dfrac{15}{24}$ ☐ $\dfrac{11}{22}$ ☐

$\dfrac{4}{22}$ ☐ $\dfrac{7}{21}$ ☐ $\dfrac{6}{12}$ ☐ $\dfrac{2}{10}$ ☐ $\dfrac{12}{24}$ ☐

$\dfrac{16}{20}$ ☐ $\dfrac{6}{6}$ ☐ $\dfrac{16}{18}$ ☐ $\dfrac{10}{14}$ ☐ $\dfrac{16}{24}$ ☐

Time: _____ Number Completed: _____ Number Right: _____

Name _____ Date _____ **Fraction Test No. 4** *(30)*

$\dfrac{14}{20}$ ▢ $\dfrac{5}{20}$ ▢ $\dfrac{9}{9}$ ▢ $\dfrac{2}{22}$ ▢ $\dfrac{2}{20}$ ▢

$\dfrac{18}{18}$ ▢ $\dfrac{4}{4}$ ▢ $\dfrac{3}{18}$ ▢ $\dfrac{2}{4}$ ▢ $\dfrac{5}{35}$ ▢

$\dfrac{2}{30}$ ▢ $\dfrac{4}{24}$ ▢ $\dfrac{10}{30}$ ▢ $\dfrac{9}{21}$ ▢ $\dfrac{30}{40}$ ▢

$\dfrac{3}{30}$ ▢ $\dfrac{10}{20}$ ▢ $\dfrac{4}{36}$ ▢ $\dfrac{6}{24}$ ▢ $\dfrac{16}{32}$ ▢

$\dfrac{15}{40}$ ▢ $\dfrac{2}{18}$ ▢ $\dfrac{7}{35}$ ▢ $\dfrac{10}{10}$ ▢ $\dfrac{4}{20}$ ▢

$\dfrac{15}{36}$ ▢ $\dfrac{4}{12}$ ▢ $\dfrac{15}{35}$ ▢ $\dfrac{10}{12}$ ▢ $\dfrac{3}{21}$ ▢

Time: _____ Number Completed: _____ Number Right: _____

178

Unit 6: Fractions in Simplest Form/One or Less
Just-a-Minute Math, SV 7940-5

$\frac{8}{8}$ ☐ $\frac{12}{30}$ ☐ $\frac{4}{6}$ ☐ $\frac{8}{32}$ ☐ $\frac{8}{24}$ ☐

$\frac{4}{6}$ ☐ $\frac{30}{30}$ ☐ $\frac{14}{16}$ ☐ $\frac{18}{36}$ ☐ $\frac{18}{30}$ ☐

$\frac{6}{14}$ ☐ $\frac{24}{32}$ ☐ $\frac{12}{20}$ ☐ $\frac{8}{40}$ ☐ $\frac{6}{21}$ ☐

$\frac{4}{10}$ ☐ $\frac{15}{30}$ ☐ $\frac{8}{18}$ ☐ $\frac{10}{16}$ ☐ $\frac{30}{36}$ ☐

$\frac{16}{22}$ ☐ $\frac{21}{28}$ ☐ $\frac{20}{20}$ ☐ $\frac{12}{14}$ ☐ $\frac{21}{36}$ ☐

$\frac{6}{28}$ ☐ $\frac{6}{10}$ ☐ $\frac{27}{30}$ ☐ $\frac{12}{21}$ ☐ $\frac{24}{30}$ ☐

$\frac{4}{30}$ ☐ $\frac{18}{20}$ ☐ $\frac{30}{35}$ ☐ $\frac{8}{10}$ ☐ $\frac{9}{24}$ ☐

$\frac{25}{30}$ ☐ $\frac{8}{14}$ ☐ $\frac{3}{36}$ ☐ $\frac{21}{21}$ ☐ $\frac{4}{32}$ ☐

STOP

Time: _____ Number Completed: _____ Number Right: _____

$\frac{3}{6}$ ☐ $\frac{2}{24}$ ☐ $\frac{6}{8}$ ☐ $\frac{4}{14}$ ☐ $\frac{14}{16}$ ☐

$\frac{12}{18}$ ☐ $\frac{8}{12}$ ☐ $\frac{20}{28}$ ☐ $\frac{3}{9}$ ☐ $\frac{8}{18}$ ☐

$\frac{18}{24}$ ☐ $\frac{8}{14}$ ☐ $\frac{27}{30}$ ☐ $\frac{10}{18}$ ☐ $\frac{6}{24}$ ☐

$\frac{2}{16}$ ☐ $\frac{9}{36}$ ☐ $\frac{8}{24}$ ☐ $\frac{14}{24}$ ☐ $\frac{8}{16}$ ☐

$\frac{10}{20}$ ☐ $\frac{7}{28}$ ☐ $\frac{6}{30}$ ☐ $\frac{10}{10}$ ☐ $\frac{16}{20}$ ☐

$\frac{10}{30}$ ☐ $\frac{4}{20}$ ☐ $\frac{9}{21}$ ☐ $\frac{15}{40}$ ☐ $\frac{3}{18}$ ☐

$\frac{4}{32}$ ☐ $\frac{18}{30}$ ☐ $\frac{24}{32}$ ☐ $\frac{25}{35}$ ☐ $\frac{7}{21}$ ☐

$\frac{5}{25}$ ☐ $\frac{2}{22}$ ☐ $\frac{3}{30}$ ☐ $\frac{3}{39}$ ☐ $\frac{10}{12}$ ☐

STOP

Time: _____   Number Completed: _____   Number Right: _____

Unit 6: Fractions in Simplest Form/One or Less
Just-a-Minute Math, SV 7940-5

$\frac{9}{5}$ ☐ $\frac{10}{4}$ ☐ $\frac{15}{5}$ ☐ $\frac{8}{5}$ ☐

$\frac{21}{7}$ ☐ $\frac{21}{9}$ ☐ $\frac{21}{3}$ ☐ $\frac{14}{12}$ ☐

$\frac{6}{2}$ ☐ $\frac{8}{3}$ ☐ $\frac{10}{2}$ ☐ $\frac{10}{5}$ ☐

$\frac{20}{12}$ ☐ $\frac{4}{2}$ ☐ $\frac{6}{4}$ ☐ $\frac{12}{6}$ ☐

$\frac{14}{7}$ ☐ $\frac{15}{9}$ ☐ $\frac{21}{14}$ ☐ $\frac{24}{9}$ ☐

STOP   Time: _____   Number Completed: _____   Number Right: _____

Unit 6: Fractions in Simplest Form/Greater than One
Just-a-Minute Math, SV 7940-5

Name _____ Date _____ **Fraction Test No. 8** *(20)*

$\dfrac{7}{3}$ ☐ $\dfrac{24}{4}$ ☐ $\dfrac{15}{10}$ ☐ $\dfrac{16}{4}$ ☐

$\dfrac{12}{2}$ ☐ $\dfrac{30}{6}$ ☐ $\dfrac{20}{4}$ ☐ $\dfrac{15}{3}$ ☐

$\dfrac{45}{15}$ ☐ $\dfrac{24}{3}$ ☐ $\dfrac{50}{15}$ ☐ $\dfrac{10}{6}$ ☐

$\dfrac{18}{10}$ ☐ $\dfrac{28}{7}$ ☐ $\dfrac{40}{20}$ ☐ $\dfrac{18}{14}$ ☐

$\dfrac{20}{5}$ ☐ $\dfrac{9}{3}$ ☐ $\dfrac{16}{8}$ ☐ $\dfrac{32}{16}$ ☐

STOP

Time: _____ Number Completed: _____ Number Right: _____

182

Unit 6: Fractions in Simplest Form/Greater than One
Just-a-Minute Math, SV 7940-5

$\dfrac{25}{15}$ ☐ $\dfrac{24}{6}$ ☐ $\dfrac{24}{14}$ ☐ $\dfrac{15}{12}$ ☐ $\dfrac{8}{6}$ ☐

$\dfrac{5}{2}$ ☐ $\dfrac{21}{6}$ ☐ $\dfrac{30}{10}$ ☐ $\dfrac{7}{4}$ ☐ $\dfrac{9}{8}$ ☐

$\dfrac{6}{5}$ ☐ $\dfrac{30}{5}$ ☐ $\dfrac{35}{7}$ ☐ $\dfrac{10}{8}$ ☐ $\dfrac{35}{15}$ ☐

$\dfrac{50}{30}$ ☐ $\dfrac{18}{3}$ ☐ $\dfrac{25}{5}$ ☐ $\dfrac{11}{10}$ ☐ $\dfrac{60}{30}$ ☐

$\dfrac{20}{14}$ ☐ $\dfrac{9}{4}$ ☐ $\dfrac{7}{2}$ ☐ $\dfrac{15}{6}$ ☐ $\dfrac{20}{8}$ ☐

$\dfrac{12}{5}$ ☐ $\dfrac{36}{18}$ ☐ $\dfrac{9}{6}$ ☐ $\dfrac{6}{3}$ ☐ $\dfrac{9}{7}$ ☐

STOP   Time: _____   Number Completed: _____   Number Right: _____

$\dfrac{13}{12}$ ☐ $\dfrac{18}{12}$ ☐ $\dfrac{5}{3}$ ☐ $\dfrac{12}{9}$ ☐ $\dfrac{12}{10}$ ☐

$\dfrac{16}{10}$ ☐ $\dfrac{50}{25}$ ☐ $\dfrac{7}{5}$ ☐ $\dfrac{24}{8}$ ☐ $\dfrac{12}{8}$ ☐

$\dfrac{18}{6}$ ☐ $\dfrac{40}{15}$ ☐ $\dfrac{27}{9}$ ☐ $\dfrac{4}{3}$ ☐ $\dfrac{8}{7}$ ☐

$\dfrac{8}{4}$ ☐ $\dfrac{24}{12}$ ☐ $\dfrac{15}{14}$ ☐ $\dfrac{10}{7}$ ☐ $\dfrac{5}{4}$ ☐

$\dfrac{8}{2}$ ☐ $\dfrac{32}{8}$ ☐ $\dfrac{20}{10}$ ☐ $\dfrac{18}{9}$ ☐ $\dfrac{16}{14}$ ☐

$\dfrac{3}{2}$ ☐ $\dfrac{14}{8}$ ☐ $\dfrac{7}{6}$ ☐ $\dfrac{16}{12}$ ☐ $\dfrac{36}{9}$ ☐

STOP

Time: _____ Number Completed: _____ Number Right: _____

Just-a-Minute Math, SV 7940-5

$\dfrac{14}{10}$ ☐ $\dfrac{21}{18}$ ☐ $\dfrac{8}{5}$ ☐ $\dfrac{7}{6}$ ☐ $\dfrac{21}{6}$ ☐

$\dfrac{36}{12}$ ☐ $\dfrac{9}{5}$ ☐ $\dfrac{5}{2}$ ☐ $\dfrac{12}{9}$ ☐ $\dfrac{10}{7}$ ☐

$\dfrac{25}{10}$ ☐ $\dfrac{12}{4}$ ☐ $\dfrac{35}{20}$ ☐ $\dfrac{18}{12}$ ☐ $\dfrac{7}{5}$ ☐

$\dfrac{10}{9}$ ☐ $\dfrac{10}{5}$ ☐ $\dfrac{40}{30}$ ☐ $\dfrac{30}{20}$ ☐ $\dfrac{40}{15}$ ☐

$\dfrac{48}{12}$ ☐ $\dfrac{8}{3}$ ☐ $\dfrac{30}{15}$ ☐ $\dfrac{18}{16}$ ☐ $\dfrac{32}{8}$ ☐

$\dfrac{22}{14}$ ☐ $\dfrac{28}{14}$ ☐ $\dfrac{12}{8}$ ☐ $\dfrac{35}{25}$ ☐ $\dfrac{20}{5}$ ☐

$\dfrac{27}{18}$ ☐ $\dfrac{40}{10}$ ☐ $\dfrac{10}{8}$ ☐ $\dfrac{45}{25}$ ☐ $\dfrac{9}{4}$ ☐

$\dfrac{40}{25}$ ☐ $\dfrac{7}{3}$ ☐ $\dfrac{7}{4}$ ☐ $\dfrac{24}{16}$ ☐ $\dfrac{5}{3}$ ☐

Time: _____ Number Completed: _____ Number Right: _____

Unit 6: Fractions in Simplest Form/Greater than One
Just-a-Minute Math, SV 7940-5

Name _____ Date _____ **Fraction Test No. 12 (40)**

$\dfrac{20}{16}$ ☐ $\dfrac{10}{9}$ ☐ $\dfrac{28}{7}$ ☐ $\dfrac{9}{4}$ ☐ $\dfrac{16}{10}$ ☐

$\dfrac{30}{25}$ ☐ $\dfrac{15}{12}$ ☐ $\dfrac{18}{6}$ ☐ $\dfrac{8}{6}$ ☐ $\dfrac{7}{6}$ ☐

$\dfrac{24}{9}$ ☐ $\dfrac{24}{12}$ ☐ $\dfrac{12}{4}$ ☐ $\dfrac{36}{18}$ ☐ $\dfrac{5}{3}$ ☐

$\dfrac{12}{6}$ ☐ $\dfrac{30}{10}$ ☐ $\dfrac{15}{3}$ ☐ $\dfrac{9}{5}$ ☐ $\dfrac{40}{15}$ ☐

$\dfrac{8}{5}$ ☐ $\dfrac{21}{6}$ ☐ $\dfrac{7}{3}$ ☐ $\dfrac{9}{3}$ ☐ $\dfrac{15}{6}$ ☐

$\dfrac{24}{8}$ ☐ $\dfrac{50}{15}$ ☐ $\dfrac{5}{2}$ ☐ $\dfrac{15}{10}$ ☐ $\dfrac{20}{12}$ ☐

$\dfrac{20}{5}$ ☐ $\dfrac{32}{16}$ ☐ $\dfrac{15}{9}$ ☐ $\dfrac{12}{5}$ ☐ $\dfrac{8}{3}$ ☐

$\dfrac{14}{8}$ ☐ $\dfrac{21}{9}$ ☐ $\dfrac{20}{14}$ ☐ $\dfrac{7}{2}$ ☐ $\dfrac{50}{25}$ ☐

Time: _____   Number Completed: _____   Number Right: _____

Unit 6: Fractions in Simplest Form/Greater than One
Just-a-Minute Math, SV 7940-5

$\dfrac{3}{2}$

$\dfrac{6}{6}$

$\dfrac{7}{2}$

$\dfrac{14}{7}$

$\dfrac{6}{21}$

$\dfrac{24}{12}$

$\dfrac{3}{9}$

$\dfrac{8}{10}$

$\dfrac{18}{21}$

$\dfrac{4}{12}$

$\dfrac{2}{14}$

$\dfrac{8}{16}$

$\dfrac{27}{9}$

$\dfrac{4}{24}$

$\dfrac{21}{14}$

$\dfrac{2}{18}$

$\dfrac{4}{8}$

$\dfrac{35}{7}$

$\dfrac{5}{25}$

$\dfrac{9}{5}$

Time: _____ Number Completed: _____ Number Right: _____

$\frac{6}{20}$ ☐ $\frac{6}{8}$ ☐ $\frac{8}{8}$ ☐ $\frac{9}{7}$ ☐

$\frac{16}{18}$ ☐ $\frac{10}{2}$ ☐ $\frac{2}{30}$ ☐ $\frac{6}{3}$ ☐

$\frac{18}{10}$ ☐ $\frac{45}{15}$ ☐ $\frac{12}{16}$ ☐ $\frac{2}{10}$ ☐

$\frac{10}{5}$ ☐ $\frac{8}{12}$ ☐ $\frac{32}{8}$ ☐ $\frac{21}{7}$ ☐

$\frac{20}{14}$ ☐ $\frac{9}{4}$ ☐ $\frac{12}{3}$ ☐ $\frac{12}{21}$ ☐

STOP

Time: _____   Number Completed: _____   Number Right: _____

Unit 6: Fractions in Simplest Form/Mixed Practice
Just-a-Minute Math, SV 7940-5

$\dfrac{4}{6}$ ☐ $\dfrac{36}{12}$ ☐ $\dfrac{2}{12}$ ☐ $\dfrac{12}{12}$ ☐ $\dfrac{35}{15}$ ☐

$\dfrac{8}{2}$ ☐ $\dfrac{15}{10}$ ☐ $\dfrac{16}{10}$ ☐ $\dfrac{6}{14}$ ☐ $\dfrac{8}{5}$ ☐

$\dfrac{21}{9}$ ☐ $\dfrac{2}{4}$ ☐ $\dfrac{15}{6}$ ☐ $\dfrac{6}{9}$ ☐ $\dfrac{15}{5}$ ☐

$\dfrac{10}{7}$ ☐ $\dfrac{3}{21}$ ☐ $\dfrac{5}{2}$ ☐ $\dfrac{40}{15}$ ☐ $\dfrac{20}{30}$ ☐

$\dfrac{6}{2}$ ☐ $\dfrac{12}{18}$ ☐ $\dfrac{15}{9}$ ☐ $\dfrac{28}{7}$ ☐ $\dfrac{6}{18}$ ☐

$\dfrac{14}{14}$ ☐ $\dfrac{20}{24}$ ☐ $\dfrac{9}{21}$ ☐ $\dfrac{10}{4}$ ☐ $\dfrac{2}{8}$ ☐

Time: _____   Number Completed: _____   Number Right: _____

$\frac{20}{12}$ ☐ $\frac{2}{40}$ ☐ $\frac{3}{24}$ ☐ $\frac{4}{10}$ ☐ $\frac{6}{10}$ ☐

$\frac{40}{20}$ ☐ $\frac{18}{36}$ ☐ $\frac{24}{9}$ ☐ $\frac{18}{24}$ ☐ $\frac{14}{21}$ ☐

$\frac{18}{6}$ ☐ $\frac{6}{16}$ ☐ $\frac{12}{9}$ ☐ $\frac{3}{6}$ ☐ $\frac{8}{18}$ ☐

$\frac{7}{14}$ ☐ $\frac{4}{20}$ ☐ $\frac{7}{3}$ ☐ $\frac{18}{22}$ ☐ $\frac{10}{25}$ ☐

$\frac{22}{22}$ ☐ $\frac{11}{22}$ ☐ $\frac{21}{6}$ ☐ $\frac{7}{28}$ ☐ $\frac{12}{5}$ ☐

$\frac{4}{14}$ ☐ $\frac{15}{24}$ ☐ $\frac{8}{3}$ ☐ $\frac{8}{14}$ ☐ $\frac{6}{24}$ ☐

Time: _____   Number Completed: _____   Number Right: _____

Unit 6: Fractions in Simplest Form/Mixed Practice
Just-a-Minute Math, SV 7940-5

$\dfrac{10}{16}$ ☐ $\dfrac{24}{8}$ ☐ $\dfrac{12}{2}$ ☐ $\dfrac{5}{4}$ ☐ $\dfrac{9}{6}$ ☐

$\dfrac{2}{24}$ ☐ $\dfrac{20}{10}$ ☐ $\dfrac{7}{21}$ ☐ $\dfrac{30}{5}$ ☐ $\dfrac{14}{12}$ ☐

$\dfrac{20}{5}$ ☐ $\dfrac{14}{22}$ ☐ $\dfrac{14}{18}$ ☐ $\dfrac{10}{18}$ ☐ $\dfrac{36}{18}$ ☐

$\dfrac{10}{6}$ ☐ $\dfrac{24}{6}$ ☐ $\dfrac{10}{8}$ ☐ $\dfrac{3}{30}$ ☐ $\dfrac{11}{10}$ ☐

$\dfrac{7}{5}$ ☐ $\dfrac{18}{3}$ ☐ $\dfrac{4}{3}$ ☐ $\dfrac{24}{30}$ ☐ $\dfrac{7}{6}$ ☐

$\dfrac{16}{24}$ ☐ $\dfrac{9}{9}$ ☐ $\dfrac{15}{14}$ ☐ $\dfrac{48}{12}$ ☐ $\dfrac{7}{4}$ ☐

$\dfrac{4}{4}$ ☐ $\dfrac{24}{14}$ ☐ $\dfrac{30}{10}$ ☐ $\dfrac{15}{30}$ ☐ $\dfrac{15}{3}$ ☐

$\dfrac{14}{16}$ ☐ $\dfrac{14}{8}$ ☐ $\dfrac{5}{3}$ ☐ $\dfrac{12}{20}$ ☐ $\dfrac{14}{20}$ ☐

Time: _____   Number Completed: _____   Number Right: _____

Unit 6: Fractions in Simplest Form/Mixed Practice
Just-a-Minute Math, SV 7940-5

$\frac{3}{18}$ ☐ $\frac{8}{24}$ ☐ $\frac{15}{12}$ ☐ $\frac{3}{2}$ ☐ $\frac{7}{35}$ ☐

$\frac{12}{24}$ ☐ $\frac{10}{12}$ ☐ $\frac{14}{24}$ ☐ $\frac{12}{10}$ ☐ $\frac{4}{36}$ ☐

$\frac{8}{4}$ ☐ $\frac{24}{3}$ ☐ $\frac{4}{28}$ ☐ $\frac{18}{14}$ ☐ $\frac{2}{16}$ ☐

$\frac{9}{27}$ ☐ $\frac{50}{15}$ ☐ $\frac{18}{9}$ ☐ $\frac{27}{18}$ ☐ $\frac{5}{20}$ ☐

$\frac{32}{16}$ ☐ $\frac{20}{4}$ ☐ $\frac{25}{15}$ ☐ $\frac{9}{8}$ ☐ $\frac{8}{6}$ ☐

$\frac{20}{8}$ ☐ $\frac{6}{12}$ ☐ $\frac{10}{10}$ ☐ $\frac{9}{24}$ ☐ $\frac{20}{15}$ ☐

$\frac{25}{5}$ ☐ $\frac{36}{9}$ ☐ $\frac{10}{20}$ ☐ $\frac{11}{33}$ ☐ $\frac{12}{4}$ ☐

$\frac{21}{3}$ ☐ $\frac{9}{3}$ ☐ $\frac{24}{4}$ ☐ $\frac{16}{20}$ ☐ $\frac{12}{14}$ ☐

STOP

Time: _____ Number Completed: _____ Number Right: _____

www.harcourtschoolsupply.com
Unit 6: Fractions in Simplest Form/Mixed Practice
Just-a-Minute Math, SV 7940-5

0.5 ☐

5% ☐

2.75 ☐

15% ☐

$33\frac{1}{3}\%$ ☐

150% ☐

0.6 ☐

0.8 ☐

1.25 ☐

0.7 ☐

0.9 ☐

0.01 ☐

25% ☐

300% ☐

10% ☐

0.2 ☐

0.75 ☐

0.25 ☐

40% ☐

23% ☐

Time: _____ Number Completed: _____ Number Right: _____

Unit 7: Fraction, Decimal, and Percent Equivalents/
Fraction Equivalents
Just-a-Minute Math, SV 7940-5

100% ☐   75% ☐   0.07 ☐   0.09 ☐

16% ☐   90% ☐   150% ☐   2.5 ☐

2.25 ☐   1.75 ☐ $0.33\frac{1}{3}$ ☐   15% ☐

0.005 ☐   0.15 ☐   70% ☐   80% ☐

0.3 ☐   20% ☐   0.1 ☐   0.5 ☐

Time: _____ Number Completed: _____ Number Right: _____

Unit 7: Fraction, Decimal, and Percent Equivalents/
Fraction Equivalents
Just-a-Minute Math, SV 7940-5

0.4 ☐   0.02 ☐   0.8 ☐   45% ☐   0.09 ☐

200% ☐   19% ☐   0.03 ☐   0.08 ☐   17% ☐

50% ☐   85% ☐   30% ☐   10% ☐   11% ☐

0.45 ☐   0.04 ☐   55% ☐   2.25 ☐   1.25 ☐

35% ☐   60% ☐   0.7 ☐   65% ☐   0.55 ☐

1.5 ☐   12% ☐   0.06 ☐   0.5 ☐   400% ☐

Time: _____   Number Completed: _____   Number Right: _____

Unit 7: Fraction, Decimal, and Percent Equivalents/
Fraction Equivalents
Just-a-Minute Math, SV 7940-5

21% ☐   18% ☐   0.95 ☐   0.85 ☐   0.7 ☐

0.75 ☐   40% ☐   0.25 ☐   2.5 ☐   1.5 ☐

0.3 ☐   0.05 ☐   20% ☐   0.1 ☐   0.03 ☐

200% ☐ $0.33\frac{1}{3}$ ☐   0.9 ☐   50% ☐   90% ☐

5% ☐   80% ☐   60% ☐   45% ☐   300% ☐

2.75 ☐   25% ☐   0.5 ☐   150% ☐ $33\frac{1}{3}\%$ ☐

Time: _____ Number Completed: _____ Number Right: _____

Unit 7: Fraction, Decimal, and Percent Equivalents/
Fraction Equivalents
Just-a-Minute Math, SV 7940-5

15% ☐   70% ☐   75% ☐   0.09 ☐   20% ☐

0.55 ☐   0.08 ☐   0.45 ☐   1.25 ☐   60% ☐

1.75 ☐   0.15 ☐   0.002 ☐ $1.33\frac{1}{3}$ ☐   1.5 ☐

13% ☐   100% ☐   125% ☐   25% ☐   2.75 ☐

0.6 ☐   0.01 ☐   5% ☐   14% ☐   40% ☐

0.4 ☐   2.5 ☐   10% ☐   0.8 ☐   0.7 ☐

85% ☐   35% ☐ $0.33\frac{1}{3}$ ☐   0.95 ☐   150% ☐

30% ☐   0.25 ☐   0.05 ☐   0.5 ☐   45% ☐

Time: _____   Number Completed: _____   Number Right: _____

Unit 7: Fraction, Decimal, and Percent Equivalents/
Fraction Equivalents
Just-a-Minute Math, SV 7940-5

22% ☐   80% ☐   1.5 ☐   90% ☐   17% ☐

0.03 ☐   10% ☐   0.4 ☐   25% ☐   125% ☐

50% ☐   0.3 ☐   0.001 ☐ $0.33\frac{1}{3}$ ☐   0.1 ☐

65% ☐ $1.33\frac{1}{3}$ ☐   5% ☐   2.5 ☐   0.06 ☐

0.05 ☐   200% ☐ $33\frac{1}{3}$% ☐   15% ☐   55% ☐

0.95 ☐   20% ☐   150% ☐   300% ☐   35% ☐

2.25 ☐   40% ☐   0.7 ☐   0.9 ☐   70% ☐

0.75 ☐   0.25 ☐   0.55 ☐   75% ☐   1.75 ☐

Time: _____   Number Completed: _____   Number Right: _____

**Unit 7: Fraction, Decimal, and Percent Equivalents/
Fraction Equivalents**
Just-a-Minute Math, SV 7940-5

$\dfrac{1}{10}$ ☐ $\dfrac{19}{100}$ ☐ $\dfrac{4}{5}$ ☐ $\dfrac{1}{5}$ ☐

150% ☐   65% ☐   16% ☐ $\dfrac{11}{20}$ ☐

$\dfrac{1}{4}$ ☐   25% ☐ $\dfrac{2}{5}$ ☐   5% ☐

20% ☐ $\dfrac{3}{10}$ ☐   75% ☐   15% ☐

33% ☐   200% ☐   70% ☐ $1\dfrac{4}{5}$ ☐

Time: _____   Number Completed: _____   Number Right: _____

Unit 7: Fraction, Decimal, and Percent Equivalents/
Decimal Equivalents
Just-a-Minute Math, SV 7940-5

$\dfrac{3}{20}$ ☐ $\dfrac{3}{100}$ ☐   50% ☐ $\dfrac{1}{1000}$ ☐

$\dfrac{3}{5}$ ☐   35% ☐ $2\dfrac{3}{4}$ ☐ $\dfrac{73}{100}$ ☐

125% ☐ $1\dfrac{1}{2}$ ☐ $\dfrac{1}{3}$ ☐   10% ☐

60% ☐   300% ☐ $\dfrac{9}{10}$ ☐ $\dfrac{1}{2}$ ☐

$\dfrac{2}{10}$ ☐ $\dfrac{7}{20}$ ☐   25% ☐   11% ☐

STOP

Time: _____ Number Completed: _____ Number Right: _____

www.harcourtschoolsupply.com

© Harcourt Achieve Inc. All rights reserved.

200

Unit 7: Fraction, Decimal, and Percent Equivalents/
Decimal Equivalents
Just-a-Minute Math, SV 7940-5

$\frac{3}{4}$ ☐ $\frac{3}{1000}$ ☐   40% ☐ $\frac{3}{5}$ ☐   1% ☐

$\frac{7}{10}$ ☐ $\frac{1}{20}$ ☐ $\frac{1}{10}$ ☐ $\frac{1}{25}$ ☐ $\frac{19}{20}$ ☐

55% ☐   85% ☐ $\frac{13}{20}$ ☐   150% ☐   75% ☐

30% ☐ $\frac{17}{20}$ ☐   21% ☐ $\frac{3}{10}$ ☐   20% ☐

90% ☐   100% ☐   80% ☐ $\frac{9}{20}$ ☐ $\frac{99}{100}$ ☐

$1\frac{3}{4}$ ☐   25% ☐ $\frac{1}{5}$ ☐ $\frac{2}{3}$ ☐   300% ☐

Time: _____   Number Completed: _____   Number Right: _____

Unit 7: Fraction, Decimal, and Percent Equivalents/
Decimal Equivalents
Just-a-Minute Math, SV 7940-5

$\frac{2}{5}$ ☐ 5% ☐ 15% ☐ 4% ☐ 225% ☐

$\frac{1}{4}$ ☐ $\frac{2}{10}$ ☐ $\frac{4}{5}$ ☐ $\frac{13}{100}$ ☐ 99% ☐

3% ☐ $1\frac{1}{4}$ ☐ $2\frac{3}{4}$ ☐ $\frac{9}{10}$ ☐ 2% ☐

26% ☐ 65% ☐ 50% ☐ $\frac{11}{20}$ ☐ $2\frac{4}{5}$ ☐

$\frac{666}{1000}$ ☐ 60% ☐ 125% ☐ 25% ☐ $1\frac{2}{3}$ ☐

$\frac{1}{3}$ ☐ $\frac{3}{20}$ ☐ $1\frac{1}{2}$ ☐ $\frac{1}{2}$ ☐ 75% ☐

Time: _____ Number Completed: _____ Number Right: _____

Unit 7: Fraction, Decimal, and Percent Equivalents/
Decimal Equivalents
Just-a-Minute Math, SV 7940-5

20% ☐   150% ☐   25% ☐ $\frac{1}{25}$ ☐ $\frac{1}{100}$ ☐

$\frac{1}{4}$ ☐   60% ☐ $\frac{3}{1000}$ ☐   125% ☐   75% ☐

200% ☐   33% ☐ $\frac{4}{5}$ ☐   14% ☐   5% ☐

$\frac{7}{10}$ ☐ $\frac{2}{10}$ ☐   30% ☐ $\frac{17}{20}$ ☐   22% ☐

3% ☐ $\frac{3}{4}$ ☐   1% ☐ $\frac{13}{100}$ ☐   90% ☐

$\frac{19}{100}$ ☐   300% ☐   18% ☐   50% ☐ $\frac{1}{5}$ ☐

$\frac{2}{3}$ ☐   55% ☐ $\frac{9}{10}$ ☐   99% ☐ $\frac{1}{2}$ ☐

24% ☐ $1\frac{1}{2}$ ☐ $\frac{3}{20}$ ☐ $\frac{3}{10}$ ☐   4% ☐

Time: _____   Number Completed: _____   Number Right: _____

www.harcourtschoolsupply.com
© Harcourt Achieve Inc. All rights reserved.

203

Unit 7: Fraction, Decimal, and Percent Equivalents/
Decimal Equivalents
Just-a-Minute Math, SV 7940-5

$\frac{1}{3}$ ☐	90% ☐	$\frac{1}{20}$ ☐	$\frac{1}{2}$ ☐	$\frac{1}{5}$ ☐
$\frac{1}{10}$ ☐	$\frac{13}{20}$ ☐	80% ☐	$\frac{1}{4}$ ☐	$1\frac{3}{4}$ ☐
65% ☐	$\frac{3}{100}$ ☐	25% ☐	20% ☐	$\frac{99}{100}$ ☐
$1\frac{4}{5}$ ☐	$1\frac{1}{4}$ ☐	$\frac{2}{3}$ ☐	$\frac{9}{10}$ ☐	200% ☐
10% ☐	$2\frac{3}{5}$ ☐	$2\frac{3}{4}$ ☐	15% ☐	$\frac{3}{10}$ ☐
$\frac{2}{5}$ ☐	40% ☐	$\frac{9}{20}$ ☐	150% ☐	$\frac{11}{20}$ ☐
100% ☐	2% ☐	50% ☐	27% ☐	$\frac{4}{5}$ ☐
35% ☐	11% ☐	$\frac{333}{1000}$ ☐	75% ☐	85% ☐

Time: _____ Number Completed: _____ Number Right: _____

Unit 7: Fraction, Decimal, and Percent Equivalents/
Decimal Equivalents
Just-a-Minute Math, SV 7940-5

$\frac{3}{5}$ ☐ % $\frac{1}{10}$ ☐ % $\frac{1}{2}$ ☐ % $1\,\frac{4}{5}$ ☐ %

0.2 ☐ % $\frac{1}{3}$ ☐ %   0.5 ☐ %   0.02 ☐ %

0.75 ☐ %   0.13 ☐ % $1\,\frac{1}{2}$ ☐ % $\frac{1}{20}$ ☐ %

0.5 ☐ % $\frac{1}{25}$ ☐ %   0.36 ☐ %   0.6 ☐ %

$\frac{2}{3}$ ☐ %   0.08 ☐ % $\frac{3}{10}$ ☐ % $\frac{73}{100}$ ☐ %

Time: _____   Number Completed: _____   Number Right: _____

Unit 7: Fraction, Decimal, and Percent Equivalents/
Percent Equivalents
Just-a-Minute Math, SV 7940-5

$\frac{2}{10}$ ☐ % $1\frac{1}{4}$ ☐ % $\frac{9}{10}$ ☐ % $\frac{17}{20}$ ☐ %

$\frac{3}{4}$ ☐ %   2.5 ☐ % $\frac{9}{20}$ ☐ % $\frac{33}{100}$ ☐ %

0.05 ☐ % $\frac{3}{100}$ ☐ %   0.18 ☐ % $\frac{4}{5}$ ☐ %

0.9 ☐ %   0.7 ☐ %   1.5 ☐ %   0.11 ☐ %

0.25 ☐ %   0.75 ☐ %   0.3 ☐ %   1.75 ☐ %

Time: _____ Number Completed: _____ Number Right: _____

www.harcourtschoolsupply.com
© Harcourt Achieve Inc. All rights reserved.
206
Unit 7: Fraction, Decimal, and Percent Equivalents/
Percent Equivalents
Just-a-Minute Math, SV 7940-5

0.1 ☐%   0.09 ☐%   0.22 ☐%   0.07 ☐%   0.38 ☐%

0.33 ☐%   2.25 ☐%   0.4 ☐% $\frac{3}{20}$ ☐% $\frac{2}{10}$ ☐%

$\frac{7}{10}$ ☐% $\frac{1}{4}$ ☐% $1\frac{3}{4}$ ☐%   0.01 ☐% $\frac{1}{25}$ ☐%

$\frac{19}{100}$ ☐%   2.75 ☐% $\frac{7}{20}$ ☐% $\frac{2}{5}$ ☐%   0.95 ☐%

0.85 ☐% $\frac{1}{5}$ ☐%   0.5 ☐%   0.8 ☐%   0.16 ☐%

0.55 ☐% $1\frac{1}{2}$ ☐% $2\frac{4}{5}$ ☐%   0.04 ☐%   1.33 ☐%

Time: _____   Number Completed: _____   Number Right: _____

Unit 7: Fraction, Decimal, and Percent Equivalents/
Percent Equivalents
Just-a-Minute Math, SV 7940-5

0.5 ☐ % $\frac{1}{3}$ ☐ % $\frac{7}{10}$ ☐ % $\frac{1}{4}$ ☐ % $2\frac{3}{5}$ ☐ %

0.03 ☐ % $\frac{4}{5}$ ☐ % $\frac{2}{3}$ ☐ % $\frac{1}{5}$ ☐ %   2.5 ☐ %

$\frac{3}{10}$ ☐ % $\frac{1}{2}$ ☐ %   0.06 ☐ % $\frac{3}{4}$ ☐ %   0.25 ☐ %

$\frac{19}{20}$ ☐ %   0.85 ☐ %   0.15 ☐ % $\frac{17}{20}$ ☐ % $\frac{9}{10}$ ☐ %

$2\frac{3}{4}$ ☐ %   2.75 ☐ %   1.25 ☐ %   0.45 ☐ %   0.6 ☐ %

0.24 ☐ % $1\frac{4}{5}$ ☐ %   0.3 ☐ % $\frac{28}{100}$ ☐ %   0.19 ☐ %

STOP

Time: _____ Number Completed: _____ Number Right: _____

Unit 7: Fraction, Decimal, and Percent Equivalents/
Percent Equivalents
Just-a-Minute Math, SV 7940-5

$\frac{5}{100}$ ☐ %　0.08 ☐ %　1.25 ☐ %　2.25 ☐ %　$1\frac{1}{2}$ ☐ %

1.33 ☐ %　1.75 ☐ %　0.21 ☐ %　0.17 ☐ %　$\frac{1}{20}$ ☐ %

0.23 ☐ %　0.12 ☐ %　$\frac{3}{5}$ ☐ %　$\frac{10}{20}$ ☐ %　0.5 ☐ %

$\frac{17}{20}$ ☐ %　0.4 ☐ %　$\frac{9}{20}$ ☐ %　$\frac{100}{100}$ ☐ %　$\frac{13}{20}$ ☐ %

$\frac{3}{100}$ ☐ %　0.33 ☐ %　$\frac{11}{20}$ ☐ %　$1\frac{3}{5}$ ☐ %　$\frac{19}{100}$ ☐ %

$\frac{2}{5}$ ☐ %　$\frac{1}{3}$ ☐ %　$2\frac{3}{4}$ ☐ %　$\frac{3}{20}$ ☐ %　0.27 ☐ %

$\frac{99}{100}$ ☐ %　$\frac{50}{100}$ ☐ %　$\frac{73}{100}$ ☐ %　0.8 ☐ %　0.04 ☐ %

$\frac{1}{10}$ ☐ %　0.01 ☐ %　$\frac{1}{5}$ ☐ %　0.95 ☐ %　2.5 ☐ %

Time: _____　Number Completed: _____　Number Right: _____

Unit 7: Fraction, Decimal, and Percent Equivalents/
Percent Equivalents
Just-a-Minute Math, SV 7940-5

0.14 ☐%   1.33 ☐% $\frac{4}{5}$ ☐%   0.09 ☐%   0.15 ☐%

2.75 ☐% $\frac{2}{3}$ ☐%   0.3 ☐%   2.25 ☐%   0.1 ☐%

0.7 ☐% $\frac{19}{20}$ ☐%   1.5 ☐% $\frac{2}{5}$ ☐% $\frac{3}{4}$ ☐%

$\frac{1}{25}$ ☐% $2\frac{4}{5}$ ☐% $2\frac{3}{5}$ ☐% $\frac{7}{20}$ ☐% $\frac{1}{5}$ ☐%

$1\frac{1}{4}$ ☐%   0.55 ☐%   0.29 ☐%   0.05 ☐% $\frac{1}{100}$ ☐%

$\frac{3}{10}$ ☐%   0.75 ☐% $\frac{13}{100}$ ☐% $\frac{7}{100}$ ☐%   2.5 ☐%

$\frac{1}{2}$ ☐%   0.02 ☐% $\frac{1}{4}$ ☐% $\frac{9}{10}$ ☐%   0.19 ☐%

0.5 ☐% $\frac{2}{10}$ ☐% $\frac{7}{10}$ ☐%   0.45 ☐% $\frac{1}{3}$ ☐%

Time: _____ Number Completed: _____ Number Right: _____

Unit 7: Fraction, Decimal, and Percent Equivalents/
Percent Equivalents
Just-a-Minute Math, SV 7940-5

Answer Key

Unit 1 - Addition

Addition Test No. 1, p. 11

1	3	7	5
8	6	8	5
9	6	7	5
2	7	6	9
4	5	8	2

Addition Test No. 2, p. 12

10	9	3	10
10	10	3	9
10	9	10	10
10	10	7	3
1	6	8	5

Addition Test No. 3, p. 13

9	8	8	9
7	4	9	6
6	9	4	7
5	2	9	10
7	8	8	8

Addition Test No. 4, p. 14

10	5	6	8
10	5	6	1
10	9	7	3
10	8	8	8
10	7	8	10

Addition Test No. 5, p. 15

9	3	7	5	9
8	9	6	9	10
5	10	7	7	2
3	4	9	6	2
7	9	7	3	10
4	7	6	9	8

Addition Test No. 6, p. 16

8	8	9	9	7
1	4	1	10	8
4	2	9	10	8
5	5	7	10	6
9	6	9	7	8
10	8	10	5	9

Addition Test No. 7, p. 17

6	5	8	6	1
4	8	7	6	10
9	9	7	10	10
8	5	9	6	8
9	4	5	7	6
2	2	3	3	8

Addition Test No. 8, p. 18

10	10	9	8	10
10	7	9	1	0
10	7	4	6	10
7	9	10	7	6
8	6	9	10	9
8	7	10	10	8

Addition Test No. 9, p. 19

11	14	11	11
14	16	16	12
12	13	12	15
15	11	11	15
14	12	17	11

Addition Test No. 10, p. 20

12	12	12	14
11	13	13	11
14	17	13	14
16	13	18	11
15	13	11	15

Addition Test No. 11, p. 21

11	11	14	13
13	12	11	14
16	11	15	11
17	13	12	13
12	13	12	12

Addition Test No. 12, p. 22

14	18	16	12
14	16	15	13
11	12	17	14
13	12	11	12
11	15	12	11

Addition Test No. 13, p. 23

11	16	11	12	13
13	14	17	12	11
13	13	12	11	12
14	11	14	18	17
15	15	13	16	16
11	14	15	12	15

Addition Test No. 14, p. 24

11	13	14	11	13
16	12	14	15	13
11	11	18	14	12
16	13	14	13	17
14	12	11	15	17
16	15	13	11	11

Addition Test No. 15, p. 25

15	11	13	16	11
12	17	11	11	18
11	13	15	12	14
12	17	14	15	15
12	13	12	11	13
12	13	16	11	14

Addition Test No. 16, p. 26

11	16	16	16	13
12	13	11	11	13
11	12	18	15	17
12	14	14	11	17
12	14	11	13	13
12	12	14	12	12

Addition Test No. 17, p. 27

6	11	10	15
8	16	9	9
6	3	7	1
9	18	11	12
7	10	4	15

Addition Test No. 18, p. 28

10	7	12	9
3	15	13	12
10	13	16	6
8	5	1	11
13	8	13	17

Addition Test No. 19, p. 29

5	5	11	8
4	8	14	16
17	14	7	13
11	10	8	10
2	11	2	5

Addition Test No. 20, p. 30

5	14	9	9
5	12	12	15
8	10	9	9
9	4	7	14
10	8	12	6

Addition Test No. 21, p. 31

7	11	6	14	11
8	7	7	8	14
14	10	16	13	2
3	12	0	12	13
4	2	12	5	2
9	6	10	11	1

Addition Test No. 22, p. 32

10	6	15	8	12
11	4	10	15	10
17	2	7	17	13
6	14	3	7	10
13	11	9	18	7
9	10	8	9	9

Addition Test No. 23, p. 33

1	7	9	8	9
6	11	14	5	8
6	12	7	18	13
15	16	4	11	9
8	5	6	7	9
16	10	12	11	12

Addition Test No. 24, p. 34

3	4	17	0	10
3	8	12	7	6
11	4	4	6	11
5	16	11	13	8
9	10	17	11	6
10	16	6	15	14

Addition Test No. 25, p. 35

7	9	6	6	8
8	8	11	9	1
16	7	11	14	16
3	3	18	14	6
9	11	1	11	5
15	13	11	4	11
15	11	4	11	7
6	9	17	14	17

Addition Test No. 26, p. 36

5	9	8	10	6
4	2	10	9	14
5	9	8	9	13
12	13	9	12	13
15	10	10	14	12
15	12	10	5	10
8	16	9	12	13
12	6	12	8	10

Addition Test No. 27, p. 37

8	7	8	11	15
7	4	14	17	7
7	7	13	0	14
5	5	11	15	3
10	2	3	9	15
7	12	4	2	10
13	15	12	9	12
10	3	13	2	6

Addition Test No. 28, p. 38

5	13	7	11	11
8	16	14	13	14
10	2	12	9	6
16	9	10	8	7
4	17	9	12	7
10	9	8	1	12
16	13	18	7	14
6	4	8	9	10

Addition Test No. 29, p. 39

9	3	5	8	7
13	8	7	15	4
1	6	15	2	8
8	13	6	13	14
12	10	6	10	14
12	7	11	9	9
9	18	17	16	9
15	12	10	11	11
10	0	10	11	12
5	5	2	6	16

Addition Test No. 30, p. 40

8	9	5	7	4
14	13	11	14	4
11	5	9	3	13
10	8	11	7	9
17	8	12	12	7
6	3	9	7	8
5	10	15	6	15
16	12	4	9	10
10	14	13	7	13
10	3	8	11	15

Addition Test No. 31, p. 41

1	6	9	14	16
5	9	12	10	16
9	15	11	8	11
11	5	14	15	8
18	14	3	16	13
12	10	17	9	8
11	8	12	13	10
8	3	9	8	13
5	11	7	7	6
9	7	6	5	13

Addition Test No. 32, p. 42

4	12	7	15	18
10	10	16	4	9
14	10	9	11	10
13	1	14	2	12
9	15	12	11	14
15	11	7	6	9
17	8	4	17	13
12	5	16	11	11
4	6	12	8	13
9	10	2	8	11

Addition Test No. 33, p. 43

5	16	14	13	7	4
7	10	8	3	10	0
11	8	11	9	7	9
17	15	11	15	16	5
13	10	17	15	9	12
11	15	9	10	12	12
14	3	9	4	7	13
10	12	11	6	10	14
13	7	13	5	12	13
14	16	10	18	10	9

Addition Test No. 34, p. 44

3	14	14	11	4	6
8	12	14	8	5	7
10	6	10	6	15	10
15	8	8	12	16	5
4	11	9	14	10	15
18	16	11	17	12	0
13	15	12	12	10	11
8	5	11	8	8	14
2	7	4	10	11	5
13	11	13	17	9	9

Addition Test No. 35, p. 45

1	13	16	7	10	12
12	7	6	14	15	15
10	11	7	12	8	12
10	9	6	13	14	14
10	6	9	8	5	2
7	8	7	13	11	2
9	12	3	11	15	12
7	17	9	1	18	13
11	9	8	16	6	6
9	13	13	3	12	14

Answer Key
Just-a-Minute Math, SV 7940-5

Addition Test No. 36, p. 46

6	12	7	13	5	13
12	7	11	14	5	16
11	10	5	14	2	6
8	5	10	11	15	14
8	14	9	17	11	13
15	13	14	7	10	10
3	16	9	8	8	12
12	9	11	11	7	16
17	8	5	12	9	15
18	9	10	9	12	3

Unit 2 - Subtraction

Subtraction Test No. 1, p. 47

5	7	0	8
2	6	4	0
2	3	2	4
3	1	5	3
2	4	8	0

Subtraction Test No. 2, p. 48

0	0	6	4
7	4	4	5
1	0	8	1
5	6	0	2
0	3	3	2

Subtraction Test No. 3, p. 49

3	1	2	1
1	1	2	1
0	5	1	2
7	6	9	3
7	5	9	6

Subtraction Test No. 4, p. 50

10	0	2	8
3	0	6	1
2	4	5	2
4	2	4	7
6	1	2	5

Subtraction Test No. 5, p. 51

4	1	2	3	3
2	7	1	2	4
5	0	0	0	2
4	5	8	6	5
0	7	2	0	5
0	6	3	3	8

Subtraction Test No. 6, p. 52

4	6	5	3	3
1	1	2	0	2
3	6	10	1	0
4	1	1	4	5
8	7	1	6	1
2	0	9	4	3

Subtraction Test No. 7, p. 53

7	4	6	8	2
9	4	6	1	1
3	0	1	8	2
3	6	0	2	6
4	1	1	5	5
1	4	4	1	3

Subtraction Test No. 8, p. 54

0	7	3	2	5
7	0	2	3	4
1	0	8	2	1
3	3	0	5	0
0	6	9	10	2
2	4	3	5	7

Subtraction Test No. 9, p. 55

4	6	6	6
9	5	5	8
9	9	8	5
5	9	4	9
7	8	6	6

Subtraction Test No. 10, p. 56

8	9	8	8
8	9	7	2
5	7	7	4
9	3	3	8
8	7	7	9

Subtraction Test No. 11, p. 57

9	5	7	8
7	9	4	8
9	4	8	7
6	6	6	8
9	8	9	7

Subtraction Test No. 12, p. 58

9	8	6	9
2	5	5	4
8	3	6	5
8	9	4	3
7	8	7	7

Subtraction Test No. 13, p. 59

9	9	2	9	5
4	8	9	8	7
7	9	8	6	6
8	7	9	9	8
7	4	8	5	5
4	6	7	7	6

Subtraction Test No. 14, p. 60

9	6	7	6	5
8	8	8	7	9
9	5	8	9	7
5	9	5	9	4
6	7	9	9	6
8	8	8	3	4

Subtraction Test No. 15, p. 61

4	7	9	4	7
8	8	8	4	5
9	6	6	2	8
7	3	9	7	9
3	8	6	5	9
8	5	7	9	5

Subtraction Test No. 16, p. 62

7	8	9	9	6
5	7	8	5	5
6	8	9	9	8
8	7	9	7	3
8	9	6	7	6
7	3	9	9	6

Subtraction Test No. 17, p. 63

2	1	1	2
2	9	2	0
6	4	8	9
8	3	8	3
5	4	9	7

Subtraction Test No. 18, p. 64

8	5	6	5
2	8	8	7
9	9	8	8
5	4	6	7
2	5	2	6

Subtraction Test No. 19, p. 65

4	7	9	3
5	2	3	2
5	6	8	7
5	0	3	6
9	8	4	0

Subtraction Test No. 20, p. 66

3	6	1	9
6	5	1	9
8	5	8	7
3	4	7	4
8	3	0	7

Subtraction Test No. 21, p. 67

8	5	9	7	4
0	4	1	1	2
6	1	8	5	2
7	3	1	7	1
7	3	7	5	1
4	9	9	7	7

Subtraction Test No. 22, p. 68

3	6	9	9	3
5	9	7	9	8
9	3	8	4	8
8	5	6	8	8
7	2	6	1	5
5	0	9	7	2

Subtraction Test No. 23, p. 69

6	8	5	5	6
3	1	0	1	5
6	5	9	4	8
3	8	2	2	6
6	4	9	3	5
7	2	3	2	4

Subtraction Test No. 24, p. 70

2	4	2	2	1
7	4	8	1	8
6	4	9	8	8
9	0	6	7	6
7	7	4	4	8
3	1	5	3	3

Subtraction Test No. 25, p. 71

2	0	2	3	4
9	6	2	6	8
3	6	6	2	9
1	9	5	1	1
8	7	5	2	4
6	2	3	9	9
3	8	4	5	4
9	7	4	6	2

Subtraction Test No. 26, p. 72

8	1	8	9	1
9	5	3	6	6
2	5	6	9	4
1	3	8	6	4
9	7	9	1	2
5	5	9	7	8
4	7	8	5	8
1	7	4	6	7

Subtraction Test No. 27, p. 73

7	6	0	8	9
8	5	5	8	4
2	9	6	3	6
2	2	9	1	8
9	2	4	2	3
8	7	7	4	9
6	4	4	7	8
4	3	0	1	3

Subtraction Test No. 28, p. 74

8	5	7	2	7
5	9	9	2	5
0	6	8	6	3
7	5	5	3	9
0	3	2	7	7
7	5	7	1	3
9	9	1	6	9
3	4	3	8	5

Subtraction Test No. 29, p. 75

7	9	8	2	7
1	8	2	2	4
2	9	1	7	8
4	1	7	3	8
9	3	3	9	3
5	6	9	7	3
6	7	5	9	8
1	4	6	3	5
5	1	4	6	2
1	9	4	3	6

Subtraction Test No. 30, p. 76

7	6	7	9	8
8	4	9	6	3
5	7	9	6	8
9	3	5	3	9
0	2	6	9	8
2	1	8	4	8
6	1	4	9	7
2	1	6	8	3
4	5	2	4	8
0	5	7	2	5

Subtraction Test No. 31, p. 77

9	9	7	5	9
5	1	4	3	6
8	5	2	2	5
4	7	0	5	8
8	1	2	4	3
7	8	1	1	7
8	7	7	4	4
2	3	9	8	5
2	7	9	8	8
2	4	8	7	1

Subtraction Test No. 32, p. 78

8	8	6	9	1
3	7	4	4	8
9	8	9	2	7
7	2	9	4	4
7	4	2	5	4
5	2	9	1	9
2	3	7	3	8
6	7	8	6	1
9	6	8	0	6
6	7	9	6	9

Subtraction Test No. 33, p. 79

9	7	4	5	1	8
9	6	2	8	3	3
9	3	2	2	6	8
3	8	1	5	0	8
4	8	5	9	9	3
4	5	5	7	9	2
4	6	8	1	1	7
1	2	5	3	8	9
2	8	6	7	4	6
3	3	3	1	6	5

Subtraction Test No. 34, p. 80

9	8	0	9	1	8
4	6	3	7	5	7
4	8	9	5	2	5
5	6	7	2	6	3
5	4	9	8	7	2
9	6	1	7	3	8
4	9	7	0	1	3
9	3	2	8	5	2
6	3	5	9	5	4
2	1	5	8	9	1

Just-a-Minute Math, SV 7940-5

Subtraction Test No. 35, p. 81

1	3	4	7	2	8
8	2	6	2	5	6
4	7	9	8	4	2
7	6	4	8	1	7
9	4	6	3	2	5
4	9	8	8	6	9
9	8	7	3	9	5
1	8	6	7	6	7
3	7	4	6	9	4
9	9	3	5	2	6

Subtraction Test No. 36, p. 82

3	8	8	4	9	8
6	1	5	8	7	8
2	3	1	6	2	6
5	9	1	9	6	8
7	2	5	9	6	5
6	9	3	6	9	9
8	6	4	9	9	7
2	2	4	7	3	6
8	7	4	4	1	7
5	3	3	3	4	5

Unit 3 - Multiplication

Multiplication Test No. 1, p. 83

8	15	7	8
30	16	0	9
5	12	28	3
4	0	27	18
24	1	0	0

Multiplication Test No. 2, p. 84

0	12	36	40
9	5	35	10
21	6	0	0
25	0	16	12
15	24	2	14

Multiplication Test No. 3, p. 85

45	20	4	9
3	0	10	6
0	4	0	0
8	18	8	15
6	32	40	35

Multiplication Test No. 4, p. 86

0	6	12	4
6	16	10	0
20	14	24	8
32	45	30	4
15	20	12	27

Multiplication Test No. 5, p. 87

15	0	6	18	7
16	15	0	12	20
4	4	0	5	18
8	27	16	30	28
0	15	12	36	24
8	32	21	1	6

Multiplication Test No. 6, p. 88

0	24	6	9	27
9	45	20	2	0
35	10	5	0	25
40	0	3	4	12
0	2	14	3	28
12	10	8	6	30

Multiplication Test No. 7, p. 89

0	10	40	12	0
20	18	21	10	45
14	18	8	5	24
6	4	8	12	16
3	4	25	0	28
30	20	9	6	0

Multiplication Test No. 8, p. 90

0	16	15	8	24
2	0	35	8	10
28	18	32	25	9
12	4	27	6	12
7	8	2	1	5
36	15	0	0	21

Multiplication Test No. 9, p. 91

18	48	0	21
49	28	63	9
8	48	42	40
27	14	32	0
0	30	45	72

Multiplication Test No. 10, p. 92

6	0	12	54
35	24	63	36
16	56	42	36
18	72	24	54
56	7	81	64

Multiplication Test No. 11, p. 93

21	36	81	54
48	63	40	9
16	32	42	0
0	18	28	42
14	8	36	56

Multiplication Test No. 12, p. 94

6	49	27	42
56	24	0	64
48	35	12	45
0	24	30	72
7	72	63	18

Multiplication Test No. 13, p. 95

0	28	49	56	48
36	42	64	27	54
72	7	16	42	40
45	72	30	63	18
18	0	63	54	81
9	6	0	0	8

Multiplication Test No. 14, p. 96

12	24	72	81	40
35	21	28	30	16
36	32	36	56	63
14	48	18	42	72
56	0	8	48	6
24	63	54	0	18

Multiplication Test No. 15, p. 97

0	24	35	54	63
32	49	7	14	16
45	56	12	63	30
27	48	24	54	8
42	36	0	0	81
64	9	21	36	18

Multiplication Test No. 16, p. 98

49	72	0	56	21
72	45	6	9	14
27	7	36	0	48
0	42	64	35	28
12	24	18	32	40
54	42	48	56	18

Multiplication Test No. 17, p. 99

0	35	14	72
35	72	6	16
12	21	0	40
0	25	4	21
27	12	45	0

Multiplication Test No. 18, p. 100

10	28	0	42
30	10	16	15
18	20	3	42
8	48	32	9
18	54	0	40

Multiplication Test No. 19, p. 101

6	1	36	7
12	16	32	0
56	24	54	63
24	15	28	18
30	8	8	0

Multiplication Test No. 20, p. 102

48	24	14	64
2	0	0	6
0	36	4	5
63	49	81	18
8	36	20	27

Multiplication Test No. 21, p. 103

0	0	3	9	24
5	24	0	48	12
56	45	54	12	27
72	0	8	36	4
0	12	28	63	36
6	9	63	0	42

Multiplication Test No. 22, p. 104

42	10	6	7	27
3	8	54	16	14
12	32	81	0	4
49	45	0	2	48
24	14	36	18	18
32	7	30	8	15

Multiplication Test No. 23, p. 105

40	10	1	21	20
16	8	72	64	15
35	35	56	16	25
18	18	30	21	28
0	0	2	0	20
40	5	9	4	24

Multiplication Test No. 24, p. 106

20	21	18	16	28
49	12	24	72	0
16	4	27	81	3
40	54	10	40	24
5	64	9	30	32
0	32	1	12	8

Multiplication Test No. 25, p. 107

0	56	8	10	36
42	3	2	63	28
36	0	63	48	14
7	45	72	45	56
36	20	8	12	27
12	0	18	4	6
35	54	6	0	30
18	15	21	15	8

Multiplication Test No. 26, p. 108

24	16	0	0	45
21	6	28	0	18
35	6	64	18	28
0	0	36	0	81
42	7	8	56	20
9	24	24	32	14
14	48	8	54	9
25	9	36	10	36

Multiplication Test No. 27, p. 109

40	63	4	6	54
48	8	16	2	20
0	4	16	40	35
4	49	12	18	63
27	7	72	32	10
0	45	27	30	21
0	49	30	15	12
72	18	12	56	12

Multiplication Test No. 28, p. 110

5	45	9	5	27
49	10	24	3	72
2	1	21	0	42
35	0	24	32	36
18	4	25	54	24
72	64	35	45	15
16	30	16	24	30
42	48	6	8	9

Multiplication Test No. 29, p. 111

2	0	24	54	81
25	45	0	8	0
72	18	18	0	42
18	10	48	35	24
16	27	7	27	20
24	0	36	24	72
10	32	12	21	9
8	30	3	36	4
16	32	0	0	14
49	54	40	40	64

Multiplication Test No. 30, p. 112

0	18	9	15	72
12	0	4	0	32
28	0	20	15	45
48	30	28	9	49
63	45	56	21	27
6	14	16	6	72
0	8	6	0	8
56	0	12	0	48
35	5	36	12	0
42	63	0	42	7

Multiplication Test No. 31, p. 113

1	18	9	27	64
42	5	0	42	3
16	8	2	14	24
21	36	24	10	14
45	27	48	3	63
54	12	32	40	81
30	20	40	10	45
18	9	20	24	15
18	4	28	36	32
6	72	12	7	54

Multiplication Test No. 32, p. 114

12	16	0	48	21
40	6	21	16	20
15	6	49	8	6
4	28	56	18	6
7	56	24	36	4
0	72	4	81	72
0	48	8	45	63
36	30	25	56	36
63	12	9	7	32
35	8	35	0	24

Multiplication Test No. 33, p. 115

24	30	64	16	2	45
42	24	18	5	28	27
28	54	6	0	21	12
6	54	16	49	35	12
0	14	18	27	16	0
6	72	18	32	3	5
56	24	48	42	10	21
36	15	25	15	30	63
8	10	8	12	20	35
14	18	63	9	8	8

Multiplication Test No. 34, p. 116

30	63	81	0	36	36
56	48	40	4	18	32
36	42	35	5	20	7
28	24	10	0	0	27
14	27	21	25	16	42
0	18	3	56	72	32
15	45	15	0	21	20
9	6	3	35	12	8
14	12	24	18	54	8
0	12	72	8	0	18

Multiplication Test No. 35, p. 117

48	6	24	24	9	45
30	6	16	42	6	21
45	0	1	72	2	4
12	7	0	0	4	15
0	16	18	36	56	81
63	24	5	64	0	9
54	10	2	9	42	30
8	4	14	0	72	32
28	49	54	32	14	20
40	0	63	56	0	16

Multiplication Test No. 36, p. 118

18	8	7	12	30	15
16	0	8	3	6	64
54	24	40	36	8	20
18	12	64	24	0	32
4	0	10	36	35	36
10	45	9	35	28	30
48	27	63	21	28	45
40	25	49	6	0	72
20	48	18	5	24	81
27	12	12	15	6	14

Unit 4 - Division

Division Test No. 1, p. 119

5	6	9	8
5	7	3	9
9	0	3	8
0	4	4	2
5	2	6	1

Division Test No. 2, p. 120

8	0	2	4
0	6	6	2
7	7	1	8
5	7	5	9
1	3	8	1

Division Test No. 3, p. 121

1	7	2	9
3	1	0	9
3	9	6	7
0	0	6	6
4	4	6	8

Division Test No. 4, p. 122

8	7	5	0
4	4	7	9
3	6	2	8
3	2	8	4
7	8	7	1

Division Test No. 5, p. 123

3	1	0	8	0
5	4	4	9	0
1	9	2	4	8
5	5	7	7	6
0	2	7	4	4
3	2	8	6	3

Division Test No. 6, p. 124

6	9	3	7	6
7	3	1	5	2
2	3	5	0	1
9	0	5	4	6
9	4	7	4	3
0	9	0	6	8

Division Test No. 7, p. 125

5	8	8	2	9
7	1	6	4	7
8	2	0	9	3
1	0	2	4	3
0	5	1	9	3
8	4	9	5	7

Division Test No. 8, p. 126

7	8	4	6	6
6	5	8	2	4
0	5	7	0	2
8	2	5	2	9
4	4	7	9	3
3	1	6	8	1

Division Test No. 9, p. 127

2	8	0	1
5	9	5	8
5	0	6	4
7	2	3	3
1	5	9	1

Division Test No. 10, p. 128

4	4	2	9
4	8	7	6
6	7	7	8
0	1	3	3
2	6	9	2

Division Test No. 11, p. 129

6	9	1	8
3	9	0	4
1	2	5	4
8	4	3	3
0	9	2	6

Division Test No. 12, p. 130

2	1	1	6
2	3	9	8
7	8	7	2
5	7	8	4
0	5	9	7

Division Test No. 13, p. 131

1	5	4	0	9
3	9	7	1	6
2	8	3	7	4
7	0	2	5	4
8	6	3	0	8
9	5	8	2	6

Division Test No. 14, p. 132

9	6	9	2	0
7	1	5	5	7
5	6	0	9	3
4	2	2	3	8
0	1	4	4	6
3	9	8	4	2

Division Test No. 15, p. 133

5	8	0	1	5
1	3	9	8	2
2	1	5	4	9
1	4	7	9	5
7	8	3	2	4
6	6	6	2	0

Division Test No. 16, p. 134

1	7	8	7	7
6	8	9	8	1
6	3	3	1	0
7	4	4	3	1
0	0	6	9	8
3	6	5	5	5

Answer Key
Just-a-Minute Math, SV 7940-5

Division Test No. 17, p. 135

6	5	9	4
7	6	7	6
8	9	4	9
9	4	3	3
0	1	0	0

Division Test No. 18, p. 136

1	2	7	3
9	8	6	2
5	9	4	9
3	6	7	7
2	7	5	0

Division Test No. 19, p. 137

6	1	0	8
4	6	5	3
8	8	1	9
8	2	6	4
8	2	4	3

Division Test No. 20, p. 138

1	5	3	7
7	5	0	1
5	8	7	3
8	4	2	6
0	0	2	5

Division Test No. 21, p. 139

1	7	2	6	4
6	0	3	8	9
5	4	6	5	8
2	6	8	2	0
9	6	0	9	4
2	0	7	1	4

Division Test No. 22, p. 140

4	9	7	5	1
3	7	8	9	1
3	3	0	9	5
1	4	7	3	4
5	6	0	4	5
8	8	3	7	0

Division Test No. 23, p. 141

2	7	3	3	3
9	9	1	0	1
6	0	0	9	1
0	2	8	2	8
7	5	2	2	6
7	4	6	5	5

Division Test No. 24, p. 142

6	6	5	8	4
6	8	9	6	10
7	7	8	0	4
6	0	1	2	8
6	0	2	3	2
9	4	3	7	5

Division Test No. 25, p. 143

4	5	5	7	6
8	9	4	9	7
4	4	5	9	2
9	7	4	9	1
0	2	3	3	0
7	2	8	0	5
1	8	1	0	3
9	0	2	3	8

Division Test No. 26, p. 144

5	4	5	8	2
6	2	2	6	6
5	9	4	8	5
8	8	9	0	7
9	6	4	7	3
0	7	8	7	4
9	5	6	9	8
7	9	5	5	9

Division Test No. 27, p. 145

3	3	0	0	0
4	0	3	0	7
1	8	2	9	7
0	2	6	5	7
6	6	3	5	5
6	9	2	4	1
8	8	4	4	3
5	7	3	3	7

Division Test No. 28, p. 146

4	9	3	0	0
4	1	3	9	5
7	9	2	2	3
9	0	5	6	3
9	8	6	5	7
6	4	9	7	7
5	7	5	9	4
8	5	7	8	6

Division Test No. 29, p. 147

7	3	6	6	7
8	7	1	9	4
8	0	9	6	5
6	0	1	5	9
6	3	3	3	0
8	4	8	8	5
6	2	3	4	2
3	9	0	7	2
6	5	7	8	7
4	5	7	5	6

Division Test No. 30, p. 148

0	4	2	6	5
9	7	1	6	5
2	7	9	4	6
7	8	5	9	7
5	3	3	9	2
2	1	5	4	6
9	8	5	2	6
8	3	3	1	8
4	5	5	7	8
2	9	8	2	7

Division Test No. 31, p. 149

7	3	5	9	2
4	4	5	5	8
7	4	7	0	7
2	7	9	4	3
0	9	1	3	1
1	2	8	7	1
6	8	9	4	4
3	8	9	6	9
3	5	3	8	2
2	4	2	6	9

Division Test No. 32, p. 150

2	3	3	3	7
4	5	3	6	1
6	5	8	9	3
5	6	2	7	4
8	1	5	0	8
5	8	5	0	9
7	4	5	1	9
1	8	4	7	5
8	9	2	3	9
6	3	2	2	4

Answer Key
Just-a-Minute Math, SV 7940-5

Division Test No. 33, p. 151

3	4	5	0	7	9
0	8	6	4	7	8
8	9	7	6	3	7
8	5	5	6	1	6
9	10	0	2	5	0
8	4	9	0	3	8
0	5	7	5	6	3
6	1	8	7	5	9
4	3	6	7	8	3
7	3	9	7	1	5

Division Test No. 34, p. 152

4	5	5	5	2	1
9	9	6	8	4	8
9	4	6	4	8	1
2	2	8	7	8	3
6	1	0	3	7	3
0	7	7	0	4	6
4	7	3	6	9	2
4	0	9	6	7	6
1	8	7	0	5	8
2	7	8	5	3	9

Division Test No. 35, p. 153

2	0	9	4	6	3
4	1	2	6	7	3
8	9	2	7	6	5
9	8	8	4	6	8
3	3	9	5	6	0
5	5	9	8	8	2
6	3	5	9	4	3
5	7	0	2	3	7
8	9	2	0	6	7
3	4	7	8	9	4

Division Test No. 36, p. 154

5	4	9	9	8	7
0	9	7	8	2	4
7	9	2	5	4	6
6	9	9	5	5	0
7	9	9	1	8	3
0	6	6	4	5	3
0	3	6	8	6	3
3	6	4	3	8	5
3	4	0	7	7	4
2	7	7	8	5	8

Unit 5 - Mixed Facts

Mixed Facts Test No. 1, p. 155

5	6	18	6
3	8	5	8
12	2	12	2
4	4	5	0
13	5	7	2

Mixed Facts Test No. 2, p. 156

14	1	30	4
0	3	7	12
45	5	15	5
2	6	4	36
15	1	56	7

Mixed Facts Test No. 3, p. 157

15	0	4	0
8	16	2	10
15	4	9	7
5	4	6	72
11	3	20	6

Mixed Facts Test No. 4, p. 158

0	1	5	11
2	28	11	7
12	4	4	8
8	13	54	4
8	4	7	10

Mixed Facts Test No. 5, p. 159

7	21	14	10	11
5	1	1	6	6
15	7	12	2	24
2	4	4	2	7
12	30	6	45	10
1	3	1	5	6

Mixed Facts Test No. 6, p. 160

6	13	42	12	27
7	7	8	3	6
7	40	6	32	10
2	4	3	1	9
12	9	20	2	7
7	5	4	5	2

Mixed Facts Test No. 7, p. 161

7	72	8	9	14
0	8	2	3	4
4	13	54	10	4
8	9	9	3	6
13	36	9	0	14
9	9	3	3	6

Mixed Facts Test No. 8, p. 162

36	14	8	11	14
5	9	2	0	6
15	35	16	0	12
1	7	4	0	3
0	9	28	13	0
3	6	3	9	8

Mixed Facts Test No. 9, p. 163

9	10	8	16	7
9	5	2	7	7
24	63	56	0	48
8	9	1	1	5
16	4	9	11	7
3	1	9	4	6
16	42	64	63	25
3	8	9	8	7

Mixed Facts Test No. 10, p. 164

5	11	12	17	12
0	2	8	8	8
18	0	27	10	35
9	1	9	9	9
18	6	17	9	5
8	2	1	3	5
40	24	0	32	18
5	6	3	2	6

Mixed Facts Test No. 11, p. 165

11	8	7	6	9
0	8	0	18	14
24	49	0	1	0
4	10	8	5	11
5	7	8	4	9
9	1	6	9	21
5	9	0	3	6
8	5	9	6	13

Mixed Facts Test No. 12, p. 166

14	14	6	8	7
5	5	3	6	9
20	28	25	21	40
7	2	7	3	7
8	9	16	13	12
4	3	4	6	1
36	42	8	0	30
3	7	7	6	5

Mixed Facts Test No. 13, p. 167

10	0	11	2	7
3	2	4	15	16
12	14	30	2	6
3	2	7	14	7
13	16	12	9	5
0	6	7	10	45
28	8	18	2	7
5	2	6	18	16
7	10	14	5	7
0	4	2	13	48

Mixed Facts Test No. 14, p. 168

8	1	8	9	8
12	24	16	24	11
5	5	9	5	1
56	9	72	9	0
4	4	6	6	4
8	64	12	8	10
3	4	5	8	6
6	1	35	12	48
4	4	8	4	6
15	27	15	42	6

Mixed Facts Test No. 15, p. 169

0	9	1	4	7
6	14	54	7	5
5	8	8	8	6
9	8	10	45	11
5	5	7	8	6
16	13	81	11	63
7	4	2	5	3
10	32	9	36	10
8	9	6	8	5
15	15	20	13	54

Mixed Facts Test No. 16, p. 170

2	9	9	3	4
10	6	12	4	7
2	7	9	3	7
15	17	9	9	35
2	7	6	0	3
6	48	5	21	7
6	8	8	9	8
36	17	24	3	56
0	8	4	9	1
11	49	12	7	18

Mixed Facts Test No. 17, p. 171

8	3	8	3	6	7
72	11	81	15	28	8
9	8	1	0	4	6
8	63	8	0	4	27
9	3	3	7	5	9
0	10	27	16	12	16
9	0	2	9	7	9
9	12	14	40	12	6
4	9	5	0	9	1
5	11	0	15	42	13

Mixed Facts Test No. 18, p. 172

3	5	4	0	8	7
30	12	12	14	56	13
0	1	0	4	6	6
7	36	11	30	14	40
7	9	6	8	3	8
36	9	18	8	32	11
6	5	5	1	9	7
13	54	16	2	13	63
7	7	9	6	7	6
24	15	18	14	24	14

Mixed Facts Test No. 19, p. 173

7	8	1	5	9	5
42	15	20	6	30	16
6	8	4	7	9	6
12	21	9	24	11	54
1	8	8	7	4	9
12	13	72	8	35	12
8	6	3	5	6	9
11	45	18	64	13	36
7	6	3	7	8	6
81	12	40	14	42	14

Mixed Facts Test No. 20, p. 174

9	5	4	9	4	6
56	13	24	14	16	13
8	8	3	9	3	4
14	56	14	32	15	16
6	8	6	7	9	7
21	11	25	7	54	8
5	8	5	6	9	8
16	49	17	14	12	18
7	7	9	4	7	8
30	17	36	9	35	9

Unit 6 - Fractions in Simplest Form

Fraction Test No. 1, p. 175

$\frac{3}{4}$	1	$\frac{1}{6}$	$\frac{1}{3}$
$\frac{1}{2}$	$\frac{1}{2}$	$\frac{1}{3}$	1
$\frac{1}{4}$	$\frac{1}{7}$	$\frac{1}{10}$	$\frac{2}{3}$
$\frac{2}{5}$	$\frac{2}{3}$	$\frac{1}{3}$	$\frac{1}{5}$
$\frac{2}{3}$	$\frac{1}{6}$	$\frac{1}{2}$	$\frac{1}{6}$

Fraction Test No. 2, p. 176

$\frac{2}{5}$	$\frac{1}{2}$	$\frac{1}{2}$	$\frac{3}{5}$
$\frac{1}{4}$	$\frac{1}{3}$	$\frac{3}{4}$	$\frac{6}{7}$
$\frac{1}{8}$	$\frac{4}{5}$	$\frac{1}{3}$	$\frac{1}{7}$
$\frac{1}{4}$	$\frac{3}{10}$	1	$\frac{1}{2}$
$\frac{1}{8}$	$\frac{1}{12}$	$\frac{2}{7}$	$\frac{4}{13}$

Fraction Test No. 3, p. 177

$\frac{1}{4}$	$\frac{7}{9}$	$\frac{5}{11}$	$\frac{1}{3}$	$\frac{3}{8}$
$\frac{5}{9}$	$\frac{2}{3}$	$\frac{1}{14}$	1	$\frac{1}{2}$
$\frac{3}{4}$	$\frac{2}{3}$	$\frac{1}{2}$	$\frac{1}{4}$	$\frac{1}{8}$
$\frac{1}{5}$	1	$\frac{2}{7}$	$\frac{5}{8}$	$\frac{1}{2}$
$\frac{2}{11}$	$\frac{1}{3}$	$\frac{1}{2}$	$\frac{1}{5}$	$\frac{1}{2}$
$\frac{4}{5}$	1	$\frac{8}{9}$	$\frac{5}{7}$	$\frac{2}{3}$

Fraction Test No. 4, p. 178

$\frac{7}{10}$	$\frac{1}{4}$	1	$\frac{1}{11}$	$\frac{1}{10}$
1	1	$\frac{1}{6}$	$\frac{1}{2}$	$\frac{1}{7}$
$\frac{1}{15}$	$\frac{1}{6}$	$\frac{1}{3}$	$\frac{3}{7}$	$\frac{3}{4}$
$\frac{1}{10}$	$\frac{1}{2}$	$\frac{1}{9}$	$\frac{1}{4}$	$\frac{1}{2}$
$\frac{3}{8}$	$\frac{1}{9}$	$\frac{1}{5}$	1	$\frac{1}{5}$
$\frac{5}{12}$	$\frac{1}{3}$	$\frac{3}{7}$	$\frac{5}{6}$	$\frac{1}{7}$

Answer Key
Just-a-Minute Math, SV 7940-5

Fraction Test No. 5, p. 179

1	$\frac{2}{5}$	$\frac{2}{3}$	$\frac{1}{4}$	$\frac{1}{3}$
$\frac{2}{3}$	1	$\frac{7}{8}$	$\frac{1}{2}$	$\frac{3}{5}$
$\frac{3}{7}$	$\frac{3}{4}$	$\frac{3}{5}$	$\frac{1}{5}$	$\frac{2}{7}$
$\frac{2}{5}$	$\frac{1}{2}$	$\frac{4}{9}$	$\frac{5}{8}$	$\frac{5}{6}$
$\frac{8}{11}$	$\frac{3}{4}$	1	$\frac{6}{7}$	$\frac{7}{12}$
$\frac{3}{14}$	$\frac{3}{5}$	$\frac{9}{10}$	$\frac{4}{7}$	$\frac{4}{5}$
$\frac{2}{15}$	$\frac{9}{10}$	$\frac{6}{7}$	$\frac{4}{5}$	$\frac{3}{8}$
$\frac{5}{6}$	$\frac{4}{7}$	$\frac{1}{12}$	1	$\frac{1}{8}$

Fraction Test No. 6, p. 180

$\frac{1}{2}$	$\frac{1}{12}$	$\frac{3}{4}$	$\frac{2}{7}$	$\frac{7}{8}$
$\frac{2}{3}$	$\frac{2}{3}$	$\frac{5}{7}$	$\frac{1}{3}$	$\frac{4}{9}$
$\frac{3}{4}$	$\frac{4}{7}$	$\frac{9}{10}$	$\frac{5}{9}$	$\frac{1}{4}$
$\frac{1}{8}$	$\frac{1}{4}$	$\frac{1}{3}$	$\frac{7}{12}$	$\frac{1}{2}$
$\frac{1}{2}$	$\frac{1}{4}$	$\frac{1}{5}$	1	$\frac{4}{5}$
$\frac{1}{3}$	$\frac{1}{5}$	$\frac{3}{7}$	$\frac{3}{8}$	$\frac{1}{6}$
$\frac{1}{8}$	$\frac{3}{5}$	$\frac{3}{4}$	$\frac{5}{7}$	$\frac{1}{3}$
$\frac{1}{5}$	$\frac{1}{11}$	$\frac{1}{10}$	$\frac{1}{13}$	$\frac{5}{6}$

Fraction Test No. 7, p. 181

$1\frac{4}{5}$	$2\frac{1}{2}$	3	$1\frac{3}{5}$
3	$2\frac{1}{3}$	7	$1\frac{1}{6}$
3	$2\frac{2}{3}$	5	2
$1\frac{2}{3}$	2	$1\frac{1}{2}$	2
2	$1\frac{2}{3}$	$1\frac{1}{2}$	$2\frac{2}{3}$

Fraction Test No. 8, p. 182

$2\frac{1}{3}$	6	$1\frac{1}{2}$	4
6	5	5	5
3	8	$3\frac{1}{3}$	$1\frac{2}{3}$
$1\frac{4}{5}$	4	2	$1\frac{2}{7}$
4	3	2	2

Fraction Test No. 9, p. 183

$1\frac{2}{3}$	4	$1\frac{5}{7}$	$1\frac{1}{4}$	$1\frac{1}{3}$
$2\frac{1}{2}$	$3\frac{1}{2}$	3	$1\frac{3}{4}$	$1\frac{1}{8}$
$1\frac{1}{5}$	6	5	$1\frac{1}{4}$	$2\frac{1}{3}$
$1\frac{2}{3}$	6	5	$1\frac{1}{10}$	2
$1\frac{3}{7}$	$2\frac{1}{4}$	$3\frac{1}{2}$	$2\frac{1}{2}$	$2\frac{1}{2}$
$2\frac{2}{5}$	2	$1\frac{1}{2}$	2	$1\frac{2}{7}$

Fraction Test No. 10, p. 184

$1\frac{1}{12}$	$1\frac{1}{2}$	$1\frac{2}{3}$	$1\frac{1}{3}$	$1\frac{1}{5}$
$1\frac{3}{5}$	2	$1\frac{2}{5}$	3	$1\frac{1}{2}$
3	$2\frac{2}{3}$	3	$1\frac{1}{3}$	$1\frac{1}{7}$
2	2	$1\frac{1}{14}$	$1\frac{3}{7}$	$1\frac{1}{4}$
4	4	2	2	$1\frac{1}{7}$
$1\frac{1}{2}$	$1\frac{3}{4}$	$1\frac{1}{6}$	$1\frac{1}{3}$	4

Fraction Test No. 11, p. 185

$1\frac{2}{5}$	$1\frac{1}{6}$	$1\frac{3}{5}$	$1\frac{1}{6}$	$3\frac{1}{2}$
3	$1\frac{4}{5}$	$2\frac{1}{2}$	$1\frac{1}{3}$	$1\frac{3}{7}$
$2\frac{1}{2}$	3	$1\frac{3}{4}$	$1\frac{1}{2}$	$1\frac{2}{5}$
$1\frac{1}{9}$	2	$1\frac{1}{3}$	$1\frac{1}{2}$	$2\frac{2}{3}$
4	$2\frac{2}{3}$	2	$1\frac{1}{8}$	4
$1\frac{4}{7}$	2	$1\frac{1}{2}$	$1\frac{2}{5}$	4
$1\frac{1}{2}$	4	$1\frac{1}{4}$	$1\frac{4}{5}$	$2\frac{1}{4}$
$1\frac{3}{5}$	$2\frac{1}{3}$	$1\frac{3}{4}$	$1\frac{1}{2}$	$1\frac{2}{3}$

Fraction Test No. 12, p. 186

$1\frac{1}{4}$	$1\frac{1}{9}$	4	$2\frac{1}{4}$	$1\frac{3}{5}$
$1\frac{1}{5}$	$1\frac{1}{4}$	3	$1\frac{1}{3}$	$1\frac{1}{6}$
$2\frac{2}{3}$	2	3	2	$1\frac{2}{3}$
2	3	5	$1\frac{4}{5}$	$2\frac{2}{3}$
$1\frac{3}{5}$	$3\frac{1}{2}$	$2\frac{1}{3}$	3	$2\frac{1}{2}$
3	$3\frac{1}{3}$	$2\frac{1}{2}$	$1\frac{1}{2}$	$1\frac{2}{3}$
4	2	$1\frac{2}{3}$	$2\frac{2}{5}$	$2\frac{2}{3}$
$1\frac{3}{4}$	$2\frac{1}{3}$	$1\frac{3}{7}$	$3\frac{1}{2}$	2

Fraction Test No. 13, p. 187

$1\frac{1}{2}$	1	$3\frac{1}{2}$	2
$\frac{2}{7}$	2	$\frac{1}{3}$	$\frac{4}{5}$
$\frac{6}{7}$	$\frac{1}{3}$	$\frac{1}{7}$	$\frac{1}{2}$
3	$\frac{1}{6}$	$1\frac{1}{2}$	$\frac{1}{9}$
$\frac{1}{2}$	5	$\frac{1}{5}$	$1\frac{4}{5}$

Fraction Test No. 14, p. 188

$\frac{3}{10}$	$\frac{3}{4}$	1	$1\frac{2}{7}$
$\frac{8}{9}$	5	$\frac{1}{15}$	2
$1\frac{4}{5}$	3	$\frac{3}{4}$	$\frac{1}{5}$
2	$\frac{2}{3}$	4	3
$1\frac{3}{7}$	$2\frac{1}{4}$	4	$\frac{4}{7}$

Fraction Test No. 15, p. 189

$\frac{2}{3}$	3	$\frac{1}{6}$	1	$2\frac{1}{3}$
4	$1\frac{1}{2}$	$1\frac{3}{5}$	$\frac{3}{7}$	$1\frac{3}{5}$
$2\frac{1}{3}$	$\frac{1}{2}$	$2\frac{1}{2}$	$\frac{2}{3}$	3
$1\frac{3}{7}$	$\frac{1}{7}$	$2\frac{1}{2}$	$2\frac{2}{3}$	$\frac{2}{3}$
3	$\frac{2}{3}$	$1\frac{2}{3}$	4	$\frac{1}{3}$
1	$\frac{5}{6}$	$\frac{3}{7}$	$2\frac{1}{2}$	$\frac{1}{4}$

Answer Key
Just-a-Minute Math, SV 7940-5

Fraction Test No. 16, p. 190

$1\frac{2}{3}$	$\frac{1}{20}$	$\frac{1}{8}$	$\frac{2}{5}$	$\frac{3}{5}$
2	$\frac{1}{2}$	$2\frac{2}{3}$	$\frac{3}{4}$	$\frac{2}{3}$
3	$\frac{3}{8}$	$1\frac{1}{3}$	$\frac{1}{2}$	$\frac{4}{9}$
$\frac{1}{2}$	$\frac{1}{5}$	$2\frac{1}{3}$	$\frac{9}{11}$	$\frac{2}{5}$
1	$\frac{1}{2}$	$3\frac{1}{2}$	$\frac{1}{4}$	$2\frac{2}{5}$
$\frac{2}{7}$	$\frac{5}{8}$	$2\frac{2}{3}$	$\frac{4}{7}$	$\frac{1}{4}$

Fraction Test No. 17, p. 191

$\frac{5}{8}$	3	6	$1\frac{1}{4}$	$1\frac{1}{2}$
$\frac{1}{12}$	2	$\frac{1}{3}$	6	$1\frac{1}{6}$
4	$\frac{7}{11}$	$\frac{7}{9}$	$\frac{5}{9}$	2
$1\frac{2}{3}$	4	$1\frac{1}{4}$	$\frac{1}{10}$	$1\frac{1}{10}$
$1\frac{2}{5}$	6	$1\frac{1}{3}$	$\frac{4}{5}$	$1\frac{1}{6}$
$\frac{2}{3}$	1	$1\frac{1}{14}$	4	$1\frac{3}{4}$
1	$1\frac{5}{7}$	3	$\frac{1}{2}$	5
$\frac{7}{8}$	$1\frac{3}{4}$	$1\frac{2}{3}$	$\frac{3}{5}$	$\frac{7}{10}$

Fraction Test No. 18, p. 192

$\frac{1}{6}$	$\frac{1}{3}$	$1\frac{1}{4}$	$1\frac{1}{2}$	$\frac{1}{5}$
$\frac{1}{2}$	$\frac{5}{6}$	$\frac{7}{12}$	$1\frac{1}{5}$	$\frac{1}{9}$
2	8	$\frac{1}{7}$	$1\frac{2}{7}$	$\frac{1}{8}$
$\frac{1}{3}$	$3\frac{1}{3}$	2	$1\frac{1}{2}$	$\frac{1}{4}$
2	5	$1\frac{2}{3}$	$1\frac{1}{8}$	$1\frac{1}{3}$
$2\frac{1}{2}$	$\frac{1}{2}$	1	$\frac{3}{8}$	$1\frac{1}{3}$
5	4	$\frac{1}{2}$	$\frac{1}{3}$	3
7	3	6	$\frac{4}{5}$	$\frac{6}{7}$

Unit 7 - Equivalents

Fraction Equivalents Test No. 1, p. 193

$\frac{1}{2}$	$\frac{1}{20}$	$2\frac{3}{4}$	$\frac{3}{20}$
$\frac{1}{3}$	$1\frac{1}{2}$	$\frac{3}{5}$	$\frac{4}{5}$
$1\frac{1}{4}$	$\frac{7}{10}$	$\frac{9}{10}$	$\frac{1}{100}$
$\frac{1}{4}$	3	$\frac{1}{10}$	$\frac{1}{5}$
$\frac{3}{4}$	$\frac{1}{4}$	$\frac{2}{5}$	$\frac{23}{100}$

Fraction Equivalents Test No. 2, p. 194

1	$\frac{3}{4}$	$\frac{7}{100}$	$\frac{9}{100}$
$\frac{4}{25}$	$\frac{9}{10}$	$1\frac{1}{2}$	$2\frac{1}{2}$
$2\frac{1}{4}$	$1\frac{3}{4}$	$\frac{1}{3}$	$\frac{3}{20}$
$\frac{1}{200}$	$\frac{3}{20}$	$\frac{7}{10}$	$\frac{4}{5}$
$\frac{3}{10}$	$\frac{1}{5}$	$\frac{1}{10}$	$\frac{1}{2}$

Fraction Equivalents Test No. 3, p. 195

$\frac{2}{5}$	$\frac{1}{50}$	$\frac{4}{5}$	$\frac{9}{20}$	$\frac{9}{100}$
2	$\frac{19}{100}$	$\frac{3}{100}$	$\frac{2}{25}$	$\frac{17}{100}$
$\frac{1}{2}$	$\frac{17}{20}$	$\frac{3}{10}$	$\frac{1}{10}$	$\frac{11}{100}$
$\frac{9}{20}$	$\frac{1}{25}$	$\frac{11}{20}$	$2\frac{1}{4}$	$1\frac{1}{4}$
$\frac{7}{20}$	$\frac{3}{5}$	$\frac{7}{10}$	$\frac{13}{20}$	$\frac{11}{20}$
$1\frac{1}{2}$	$\frac{3}{25}$	$\frac{3}{50}$	$\frac{1}{2}$	4

Fraction Equivalents Test No. 4, p. 196

$\frac{21}{100}$	$\frac{9}{50}$	$\frac{19}{20}$	$\frac{17}{20}$	$\frac{7}{10}$
$\frac{3}{4}$	$\frac{2}{5}$	$\frac{1}{4}$	$2\frac{1}{2}$	$1\frac{1}{2}$
$\frac{3}{10}$	$\frac{1}{20}$	$\frac{1}{5}$	$\frac{1}{10}$	$\frac{3}{100}$
2	$\frac{1}{3}$	$\frac{9}{10}$	$\frac{1}{2}$	$\frac{9}{10}$
$\frac{1}{20}$	$\frac{4}{5}$	$\frac{3}{5}$	$\frac{9}{20}$	3
$2\frac{3}{4}$	$\frac{1}{4}$	$\frac{1}{2}$	$1\frac{1}{2}$	$\frac{1}{3}$

Fraction Equivalents Test No. 5, p. 197

$\frac{3}{20}$	$\frac{7}{10}$	$\frac{3}{4}$	$\frac{9}{100}$	$\frac{1}{5}$
$\frac{11}{20}$	$\frac{2}{25}$	$\frac{9}{20}$	$1\frac{1}{4}$	$\frac{3}{5}$
$1\frac{3}{4}$	$\frac{3}{20}$	$\frac{1}{500}$	$1\frac{1}{3}$	$1\frac{1}{2}$
$\frac{13}{100}$	1	$1\frac{1}{4}$	$\frac{1}{4}$	$2\frac{3}{4}$
$\frac{3}{5}$	$\frac{1}{100}$	$\frac{1}{20}$	$\frac{7}{50}$	$\frac{2}{5}$
$\frac{2}{5}$	$2\frac{1}{2}$	$\frac{1}{10}$	$\frac{4}{5}$	$\frac{7}{10}$
$\frac{17}{20}$	$\frac{7}{20}$	$\frac{1}{3}$	$\frac{19}{20}$	$1\frac{1}{2}$
$\frac{3}{10}$	$\frac{1}{4}$	$\frac{1}{20}$	$\frac{1}{2}$	$\frac{9}{20}$

Fraction Equivalents Test No. 6, p. 198

$\frac{11}{50}$	$\frac{4}{5}$	$1\frac{1}{2}$	$\frac{9}{10}$	$\frac{17}{100}$
$\frac{3}{100}$	$\frac{1}{10}$	$\frac{2}{5}$	$\frac{1}{4}$	$1\frac{1}{4}$
$\frac{1}{2}$	$\frac{3}{10}$	$\frac{1}{1000}$	$\frac{1}{3}$	$\frac{1}{10}$
$\frac{13}{20}$	$1\frac{1}{3}$	$\frac{1}{20}$	$2\frac{1}{2}$	$\frac{3}{50}$
$\frac{1}{20}$	2	$\frac{1}{3}$	$\frac{3}{20}$	$\frac{11}{20}$
$\frac{19}{20}$	$\frac{1}{5}$	$1\frac{1}{2}$	3	$\frac{7}{20}$
$2\frac{1}{4}$	$\frac{2}{5}$	$\frac{7}{10}$	$\frac{9}{10}$	$\frac{7}{10}$
$\frac{3}{4}$	$\frac{1}{4}$	$\frac{11}{20}$	$\frac{3}{4}$	$1\frac{3}{4}$

Decimal Equivalents Test No. 1, p. 199

0.1	0.19	0.8	0.2
1.5	0.65	0.16	0.55
0.25	0.25	0.4	0.05
0.2	0.3	0.75	0.15
0.33	2	0.7	1.8

Decimal Equivalents Test No. 2, p. 200

0.15	0.03	0.5	0.001
0.6	0.35	2.75	0.73
1.25	1.5	$0.3\overline{3}$	0.1
0.6	3	0.9	0.5
0.2	0.35	0.25	0.11

Decimal Equivalents Test No. 3, p. 201

0.75	0.003	0.4	0.6	0.01
0.7	0.05	0.1	0.04	0.95
0.55	0.85	0.65	1.5	0.75
0.3	0.85	0.21	0.3	0.2
0.9	1	0.8	0.45	0.99
1.75	0.25	0.2	$0.6\overline{6}$	3

Decimal Equivalents Test No. 4, p. 202

0.4	0.05	0.15	0.04	2.25
0.25	0.2	0.8	0.13	0.99
0.03	1.25	2.75	0.9	0.02
0.26	0.65	0.5	0.55	2.8
0.666	0.6	1.25	0.25	$1.6\bar{6}$
$0.3\bar{3}$	0.15	1.5	0.5	0.75

Decimal Equivalents Test No. 5, p. 203

0.2	1.5	0.25	0.04	0.01
0.25	0.6	0.003	1.25	0.75
2	$0.3\bar{3}$	0.8	0.14	0.05
0.7	0.2	0.3	0.85	0.22
0.03	0.75	0.01	0.13	0.9
0.19	3	0.18	0.5	0.2
$0.6\bar{6}$	0.55	0.9	0.99	0.5
0.24	1.5	0.15	0.3	0.04

Decimal Equivalents Test No. 6, p. 204

$0.3\bar{3}$	0.9	0.05	0.5	0.2
0.1	0.65	0.8	0.25	1.75
0.65	0.03	0.25	0.2	0.99
1.8	1.25	$0.6\bar{6}$	0.9	2
0.1	2.6	2.75	0.15	0.3
0.4	0.4	0.45	1.5	0.55
1	0.02	0.5	0.27	0.8
0.35	0.11	0.333	0.75	0.85

Percent Equivalents Test No. 1, p. 205

60	10	50	180
20	33	50	2
75	13	150	5
50	4	36	60
67	8	30	73

Percent Equivalents Test No. 2, p. 206

20	125	90	85
75	250	45	33
5	3	18	80
90	70	150	11
25	75	30	175

Percent Equivalents Test No. 3, p. 207

10	9	22	7	38
33	225	40	15	20
70	25	175	1	4
19	275	35	40	95
85	20	50	80	16
55	150	280	4	133

Percent Equivalents Test No. 4, p. 208

50	$33\frac{1}{3}$	70	25	260
3	80	$66\frac{2}{3}$	20	250
30	50	6	75	25
95	85	15	85	90
275	275	125	45	60
24	180	30	28	19

Percent Equivalents Test No. 5, p. 209

5	8	125	225	150
133	175	21	17	5
23	12	60	50	50
85	40	45	1	65
3	33	55	160	19
40	$33\frac{1}{3}$	275	15	27
99	50	73	80	4
10	1	20	95	250

Percent Equivalents Test No. 6, p. 210

14	133	80	9	15
275	$66\frac{2}{3}$	30	225	10
70	95	150	40	75
4	280	260	35	20
125	55	29	5	1
30	75	13	7	250
50	2	25	90	19
50	20	70	45	$33\frac{1}{3}$

Answer Key
Just-a-Minute Math, SV 7940-5

It's TIME to certify that

_____

has shown GREAT IMPROVEMENT in

_____

Teacher

Tick-Tock! You Rock!

_____

You are now a member of the
1 Minute Club
for

_____

Teacher

Award Certificates
Just-a-Minute Math, SV 7940-5